BUS3060

Fundamentals of Finance and Accounting

Selected material from

FINANCE FOR NON-FINANCIAL MANAGERS

Gene Siciliano

CAPELLA UNIVERSITY

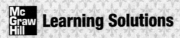
Learning Solutions

Boston Burr Ridge, IL Dubuque, IA New York San Francisco St. Louis
Bangkok Bogotá Caracas Lisbon London Madrid
Mexico City Milan New Delhi Seoul Singapore Sydney Taipei Toronto

BUS3060
Fundamentals of Finance and Accounting

10 11 MER   12 1 1

ISBN 0-07-326077-0

Custom Publishing Specialist: Shirley Grall
Production Editor: Jessica Portz
Printer/Binder: Mercury Print Productions

Contents

Financing the Business

Preface

W hy should you buy this book? There are certainly others to choose from, each with a viewpoint that reflects the author's background and opinions. Why this one? Why this particular author's background and opinions? The answer is *communication*: this book is in a sense a communication manual for non-financial managers.

I believe there is a great need for better communication between financial and non-financial professionals, for a better tool to help the non-financial manager understand the language of finance, and for the financial professional to learn the terminology that has meaning for the non-financial manager. I believe this book will play a part in enabling that better communication. That is, in fact, its purpose.

Why me? I spent eight years of my early working life as a practicing CPA. I felt the frustration that came from not speaking the same language as my clients and the difficulty in getting the information I needed from people who didn't really understand why I could possibly need it or what I could do with it. Then there were the 14 years as a financial officer inside several companies, responsible for trying to find a common language so I could provide business managers what they needed to run their departments, divisions, and corporations. Most recently, I have spent over 15 years as an advisor to business managers and entrepreneurs on financial matters.

Over each of those phases of my career, I've become known for my ability to translate complex or esoteric financial concepts into plain language. I understand better than most both the accountant's and the business manager's viewpoints. Not surprisingly, they often speak different languages. The results are usually less than satisfactory for both. This book is my attempt to facilitate a better understanding between them, since their common objective is the greater success of the enterprise that employs them both.

What should you hope to get from this book, or any book on this subject? I believe the answer is:

- The viewpoint of an author who speaks the language of finance, but thinks more like a line manager than an accountant,
- Examples of the typical, standard financial reports, with plenty of explanation—in English—that will help you understand those same kinds of reports when you see them in your company,
- Examples of financial reports you may not see in your company yet, but that you might want to, because they could give you valuable information, and
- Some help in mastering the tools of finance where they can be useful to you, without wasting time explaining the deep details that will likely never benefit you.

If you are now or intend to become, at some point in your career, the manager in charge of a profit center or perhaps the owner of your own business, you will need to have a working knowledge of a lot of the information in this book. You are or may become:

- The person your staff looks to for guidance in budgets and other financial management matters,
- The person your boss or the home office expects to consistently achieve your assigned financial targets—or even the person who sets those targets,
- The person who is responsible for directing the finance and accounting function that supports your unit or company, and
- The person who can effectively explain to staff, boss,

board of directors, and perhaps even outsiders the financial implications of the results you have achieved and the
results you expect to deliver in the future.

Regardless of your path, your career success depends on
your doing these things reasonably well, and you cannot do that
without a respectable knowledge of finance and accounting.
Notice I didn't say a *thorough* knowledge and I didn't say you
need to understand how accountants process detailed information. I didn't even say you had to get it right every time,
because accountants don't either. But you do need to be comfortable talking the language of finance at the nontechnical
level, so that you can communicate effectively in either direction. And that is the purpose of this book.

How to Use This Book

Chapter 1 sets the stage for the book. It discusses how events in
the business world today have increased the need for financially
savvy managers. Business managers and owners today need to
have both financial integrity and a degree of financial compe-
tence not previously expected of them. It is no longer good
enough to keep poor accounting records in the belief that the
accountants will clean it all up at the end of the year, so the
company can file correct tax returns. It is no longer good enough
to scan a financial report to find the profit number for the month,
so that the rest of the report may be ignored. It is no longer good
enough for a manager to be ignorant of financial terminology if
he or she wants to climb the corporate ladder, or even be
demonstrably successful in a current job. You need more.

Chapters 2 through 6 cover the basic financial reports you
should typically see on a monthly basis, with lots of tips on
reading, understanding, and using the information they contain.
For that reason we suggest that, as your first objective, you
read, and perhaps reread, Chapters 2 through 6 in order, until
you feel comfortable with them.

Then we suggest you proceed to Chapters 7 and 8, which

delve into the "hidden information" that every company has. Each is intended to explore a specific analysis area in which basic financial information is reorganized and detailed in more depth in order to present that hidden information. The objective of these chapters is for you to know how to get to that information from these reports *and* understand what the reports are telling you.

Chapter 7 focuses on operating ratios, selected relational calculations based on numbers in the financial statements. Their purpose is to show relationships between two variables that may not be visible in a casual reading of the statements, but that are important to assessing a company's overall financial health. We will discuss some of the most common and useful ratios and how you can best use them to better understand the underlying strength of whatever it is they are measuring. This is a chapter you might return to often, as it is a handy reference tool.

Chapter 8 explains the essentials of cost accounting—how it works and why it is so important in helping a company control its gross profit margins. The fundamental purpose of cost accounting is to enable managers to know the actual cost of the products or services their company sells, so they can choose to sell more of the profitable ones and less of the unprofitable ones.

Chapter 9 is about business planning. It discusses the importance of planning, the difference between strategic planning and operational planning, using vision and mission as the starting point for planning strategy, and setting long-term and short-term goals.

Chapter 10 explains the fundamentals of financing a business—getting the capital to launch it and the working capital to operate it. This is an important area for growing businesses everywhere, because growth consumes capital often at a faster rate than a growing business can create it internally. This chapter looks at both debt and equity financing, explains some of the techniques used, and discusses some of the advantages and disadvantages of each.

Chapters 11 and 12 explore the critical management function of planning, including operational planning and budgeting. These sections are placed last so that you first get an understanding of the things you typically plan for—profits, cash flow, and financing the business—before you get into the planning itself.

It's my hope that you'll refer to sections of this book many times over, long after you have finished the first read. By using this book as an ongoing reference, you will reinforce the lessons it contains and find new ways to use it with each reading.

Special Features

The idea behind the books in the Briefcase Series is to give you practical information written in a friendly, person-to-person style. The chapters deal with tactical issues and include lots of examples. They also feature numerous boxes designed to give you different types of specific information. Here's a description of the boxes you'll find in this book.

These boxes do just what they say: give you tips and tactics for using these ideas to understand and use financial information to manage intelligently.

These boxes provide warnings for where things could go wrong when you're getting involved in financial analysis and transactions.

These books give you how-to hints for collecting, analyzing, and using financial information.

Every subject has some special jargon and terms—finance more than most. These boxes provide definitions of these terms.

It's always useful to have examples that show how the principles in the book are applied. Learn how others apply them in these boxes.

 This icon identifies boxes where you'll find specific procedures you can follow to take advantage of the book's advice.

 How can you make sure you won't make a mistake with financial matters? You can't, but these boxes will give you practical advice on how to minimize the possibility of an error.

Acknowledgments

I long ago told myself that writing a book would be a lot of work, and I already had plenty of work without taking on a book project. My thanks to John Woods of CWL Publishing Enterprises for making me an offer I couldn't refuse, in order to get this book out of my head and on to paper. It needed writing, and I knew I had to write it sooner or later. This was the best of times, thanks to John.

Sometimes what I wrote was clear and concise, and sometimes it wasn't even close. I appreciate those people who helped me with editing the material so that my intended audience would more easily understand what I was trying to say. I want to thank Bob Magnan, whose job it was to make my streams of consciousness more readable. I am particularly indebted to Daniel Feiman and Ed Story, two gifted associates of mine who lent their talents to improving the quality of the content and the clarity of the grammar in several key chapters.

Finally, all those efforts would have been in vain if my beloved partner, Karen Dellosso, hadn't been willing to let me stretch already very long workdays into even longer workdays as this book came into form.

Thank you all. I really appreciate you.

About the Author

Gene Siciliano, CMC, CPA, is a financial management consultant. His business is helping companies increase profits and cash flow by raising their financial awareness and employing best management practices. His tools of the trade include business planning and modeling, financial department effectiveness audits, board service, management coaching, and a series of training and workshop programs, largely focused on finance and accounting for predominantly non-financial clients.

An active member of the National Speakers Association and an avid communicator, Gene speaks to corporate and association audiences nationwide on financial and management topics. His articles on financial management, business planning, and cost control have been published internationally. He also publishes an electronic newsletter for managers of privately owned companies entitled *We Thought You'd Like to Know*.

Following graduation from Penn State University's Smeal College with a business degree in accounting, Gene spent several years on active duty as a Naval Reserve officer. He carries the permanent rank of Commander, U.S. Navy—Retired. Returning to civilian life, he joined Alexander Grant & Company (now Grant Thornton), a large public accounting firm. After nearly eight years as a practicing CPA, he entered the corporate world, where he held senior financial management positions with Computer Sciences Corporation, Epson America, and several smaller companies. In 1986 he founded Western Management Associates, the consulting business that he owns and operates today. In his practice he often serves as the part-time chief financial officer for client companies. From that experience grew the trademark of his business, Your CFO for Rent.®

When not in the office, Gene has served nonprofit organizations—both professional and charitable—as president, board member, and treasurer. He is most often drawn to organizations that help children. In his spare time, he enjoys tennis and the theater, both available in abundance near his home in Redondo

Beach, California. He can be reached at 310 645-1091 or gene@CFOforRent.com or by visiting his Web site at www.CFOforRent.com.

Structure and Interrelationship
of Financial Statements

Counting the Beans:
How Critical Is Good Financial Information, Anyway?

The members of every generation believe the business environment in which they work is tougher than ever before. Today we are no exception. Those who follow us will likely be no exception. Well, guess what? Everybody's right!

Managing a Company in Today's Business Environment

As business gets more competitive, more global, more technologically driven, it gets easier for others to compete with you. It gets harder to be successful by just doing OK. It gets harder to launch a good product and enjoy the benefits of your innovation for a long time without serious competition. And, yes, it does get tougher to make a living. So what was good enough for our parents to be able to get by and make a "good living" isn't good enough today. You may have read that many of us will fail to achieve the relative standard of living that our parents did because of that tougher world out there. Of course, if you've been alive for the past 10 or 15 years, you also know that there are unprecedented opportunities to create new wealth, new products, new companies, and new fortunes that never before existed. It's unlikely that our forefathers could have imagined fortunes being made, and lost, as quickly as they were in the '90s.

So it's hard to argue that times are more challenging now. The question is: what can you do about it? The answer: not much about the times, but a lot about how you prepare for them. And that's what this book is all about.

When I was a young boy, my father owned and ran a small grocery store that supplied the neighbors with their daily household needs, long before supermarkets killed the mom-and-pops that then existed in every neighborhood. When school was over, I went to the store to help out, because mom and dad were both working there. My first job was opening cases of packaged goods, pricing the packages, and stocking the shelves. Then I packed groceries and delivered them to customers, sometimes after taking their order over the phone and personally filling it. (Yes, that was how many small stores did business back then.) Then I graduated to cutting meat in the fresh meat department. By the time I was in junior high school, I was checking out customers, opening the store in the morning, and finally running the store when my parents went on a rare vacation. By the time I was in high school, I had run every aspect of a small business, including opening and closing the cash register and doing the bookkeeping at the end of the day.

In today's business terms, I had worked in shipping/receiving, warehousing and inventory control, production, sales, delivery, billing and collection, accounting, and management.

Uncommon today? Yes, and yet that diverse background is exactly what is being demanded more and more of today's up-and-coming professionals. Managers in companies large and small, including directors, vice presidents, and general managers, are finding their particular specialties aren't going to carry them to the finish line as they might once have.

Their first clue might have been the arrival of the personal computer. Senior managers and company executives a generation ago were challenged by their lack of knowledge of this new tool, no matter how firmly they knew their own particular areas of expertise. The young professionals coming into the business often made their bosses look old-fashioned with their mastery of this impressive and intimidating technology. Soon, as we discovered, those young professionals had children, whose computer acumen after being on the planet for only a few years made even their savvy parents sit up and take notice. And so it goes.

Now, as we are learning, finance and accounting are having an impact on many companies in ways never before thought of by managers outside the financial department. The accounting scandals of 2002 showed that financial incompetence, or carelessness, or simply lack of integrity, could wipe out the efforts of thousands of loyal, hard-working employees. The report card, it seems, has become more important than it ever was when we were in school.

Today we're finding out that we need to know how to read a report card so we can just keep our jobs, let alone advance in our careers. Boards of directors now need to delve into the reports they have routinely received for years to a degree never before contemplated. They need to understand financial terminology and accounting methods they might previously have taken for granted. CEOs now need to be completely aware of what their people are doing and the financial ramifications, because they will no longer be able to credibly say they didn't know. And finally, managers within a company, whether large or small, are going to need to understand the rules of accounting and the boundaries of proper finance well enough to avoid getting into trouble just because they were aggressively trying to make their goals. As for those who aspire to become managers, they might not even get started up the ladder until they can demonstrate this kind of knowledge. So you see, it touches everyone.

Now, it's all well and good to say that accounting scandals will make everyone learn more about finance and accounting, but is that the only reason to know this stuff? Of course not!

4

Budget A projection of the detailed income and expenses that we estimate will occur in a future period, usually prepared on a month-to-month basis for up to a year. Each kind of income and expense is listed, along with the amount each line is expected to add to or subtract from the profit for the period.

Consider the new manager who is asked to prepare a budget for his or her department.

How do you begin your budget? Well, how about sales? Do you start with what you hope you can sell? What you're sure you can sell? What you sold last year or last month? What will management believe?

OK, if that's too confusing, maybe you should start with expenses. What do you need to spend? What you spent last year or last month? What you hope you can get approval to spend? Do you actually know what it will really cost?

Just knowing where to begin is a challenge. And then how do you decide how much money or staffing you'll need to reach the goals you want to achieve or that your boss wants you to achieve?

Whew! Why can't Finance just do this for you?

And the truth is, of course, they really can't. Oh, sure, Finance can prepare something that looks like a budget and in many companies that's what happens. But then it's not really your budget; it's theirs. And if you miss the target they set, well, it's not really your problem, now, is it? Yet as managers we know that each department knows its unique needs and capabilities better than anyone else. And we know from Management 101 that a goal must be accepted—better yet, owned—by the people who actually will do the work, for there to be a strong commitment to achieving it. And that, simply put, is why each department within the organization must do its own budget and, therefore, why its managers must learn to budget effectively. And, yes, you will need to be able to answer, at some level, all the questions I've raised above. Happily, Chapter 10 in this book will help you do that.

The Role of the Finance Department

The Finance Department really has two fairly distinct jobs to perform in most companies: managing the company's financial resources ("Finance") and recording and reporting all its financial transactions ("Accounting"). Many of today's mid-sized and smaller companies don't establish separate Finance and Accounting departments within their organizations. A company might instead have a chief financial officer who per-

forms or oversees the finance functions for the company and oversees the company's accounting activities. Larger companies will usually be fairly precise about their organization and are likely to have distinctly separate departments reporting to the CFO.

> **Chief financial officer (CFO)** The job title of the executive who is in overall charge of all the financial department activities in all large companies and most mid-sized ones. Smaller companies might instead place their financial department under a vice president for finance or even a controller, depending on how they define the responsibilities of these people.

Finance

The Finance Department can be an accumulation of diverse functions, depending on the company. It may oversee such areas as insurance and risk management, contract administration and pricing, internal auditing, investor relations, and more. But at a minimum, Finance will likely be responsible for treasury activities, often under an executive carrying the title of treasurer or vice president for finance. His or her role will likely include cash management, bank relations, investments, and everything having to do with making sure the organization has enough cash to do its job and has all its cash busily working or productively invested.

Major activities like mergers and acquisitions, attracting investors to a company seeking outside capital, and internal management of public stock offerings—all traditional roles of Finance—will usually fall within the Finance Department's

---

⚠ CAUTION! ⚠

Don't Judge the Executive Book by Its Cover

While we have tried to give you a general idea of what job titles might do which jobs, these are generalizations that do not apply to every company, and maybe not yours. Some companies are more liberal than others in granting titles. Still others might employ little-used titles such as "director of finance" or "vice president of administration" or even "manager of accounting" to indicate the head financial executive in their organization. It's best to obtain an organization chart or ask someone in Human Resources or the Finance Department when determining exactly who does what. It could save you embarrassment or, even worse, getting the wrong information.

---

responsibility. A company that decides to take its stock to the public marketplace for the first time—in an initial public offering (IPO)—will almost always place the coordination role for that transaction in the hands of the Finance Department.

Accounting

The accounting job is typically done by the Accounting Department, led by an accounting manager, controller, comptroller, or similar title. These folks record all the transactions that occur as the company does its business and then prepare reports that help them, company management, and outside constituencies understand the financial impact of those transactions.

The accountants maintain the accounting software, process all the paperwork that documents transactions that have occurred, and record them into the company's general ledger. Most of these transactions are recorded in dollars and cents, or the appropriate foreign currency for operations outside the U.S. Some transactions keep track of other units of measure besides currency, such as the number of pieces of inventory in the warehouse, the number of vehicles in the company fleet, and so on.

Of course, keeping records of financial transactions tucked away in some computer serves no one unless we can get access to the information when we need it. So, from all those transaction records the accountants are able to prepare a variety of reports. Some are for people outside your company, like the government, your bankers, investors, and stockholders. But most important to running the company are the reports the accountants prepare for company managers, for it is those reports that managers use to understand their company's financial past and make decisions about its financial future.

> **General ledger** The principal accounting record into which all transactions of the company are recorded and summarized. The general ledger is the record from which information for the basic financial reports is drawn. It varies greatly in appearance. These were once huge books maintained with carefully handwritten entries, but nearly all general ledgers today are produced by computer software.

As you will learn later in this book, or as you may already have discovered the hard way, the readability of those reports is a huge factor in their value. Put another way, it's hard to use a report you can't understand, no matter how valuable the information it contains.

That, unfortunately, is the way some managers view the basic financial reports their companies' computerized accounting programs typically produce. (We'll discuss these reports in depth in Chapters 3 and 4.) Managers often have good reason to feel that way, it seems to me, because these basic financial reports were designed primarily for use by outsiders! Their purpose is to give a snapshot of a company's financial condition to people outside the company—bankers, government regulators, stock analysts, investors, and others who have no direct role in running the company. While that may be true, these reports still provide an essential summary of the company's monthly or quarterly operations in a standard format that is consistent and familiar, thus making them more credible and useful. They also serve as the basis for more tailored and typically more useful reports, which we'll discuss later on in this book.

GAAP: The "Rules" of Financial Reporting

The standard format for recording and reporting financial trans-

You Don't Get What You Don't Ask For

Smart Managing Some accounting departments produce reports that they never distribute outside their department, because no one has ever asked for them. These reports, perhaps produced as part of a standard computerized process or to serve a limited purpose in Accounting, might contain information you have been trying to collect on the back of an envelope for months. If they don't know you want it, they're not likely to go looking for you when it's printed. Ask what kinds of reports are produced that don't get distributed, just in case there is a gem hidden in that file cabinet. Of course, this also applies to reports that aren't printed but are accessible through your computer network.

actions is outlined in guidelines, or rules, called *Generally Accepted Accounting Principles* (GAAP). These guidelines are published by the accounting profession (with some gentle help from the U.S. government). They are intended to be the foundation upon which report readers can gauge a company's progress, compare one company or one accounting period with another, and generally judge the financial effectiveness of its management efforts.

Key Term

Generally Accepted Accounting Principles (GAAP) A set of rules, conventions, standards, and procedures established by the Financial Accounting Standards Board for reporting financial information.

As we've seen, it doesn't always work out that way, but that's not necessarily because the rules are flawed. The job of creating comparable accounting and reporting standards for businesses as widely varied as those operating today can be a daunting task for the folks who set the standards. The objective of each accounting rule is to record a transaction so that it makes economic sense for the company and for readers of the company's reports. Yet to achieve that objective, accountants in two dissimilar companies might need to record the same transaction differently.

We will devote a fair amount of time in this book to helping

Are All Fords Created Equal?

Two companies purchase identical Ford Taurus automobiles. Company A will use its vehicle for occasional corporate visitors, so it's expected to last about five years. Company B will use its vehicle as part of its fleet of taxis, so it's expected to last about 18 months. Over which of the following periods of time would an accountant depreciate or expense the purchase?

1. five years
2. 18 months
3. three years (an average)
4. different lives in different companies, based on their actual useful life in those companies

The choice will affect the profits of any company that buys cars. The choices that companies must make to reflect their particular realities might lead to confusion and misstatement. However, setting one absolute rule for all companies would create different confusion, perhaps greater. Thus arose the concept of generally accepted accounting principles, rather than absolute rules. These principles have been the basis for reasonable estimates and unreasonable abuses for many years, with the abuses getting a lot more press as this is written.

Incidentally, the answer is 4.

---

you understand how to read and use these primary financial statements, prepared in accordance with GAAP. We will also discuss other, special-purpose reports that company management may find more useful for internal purposes. Our comments will in all cases assume the use of GAAP, except where we specifically note exceptions.

The Relationship of Finance and Accounting to the Other Departments

The Finance Department in every company has in theory two primary areas of responsibility:

- To safeguard the assets of the company by properly accounting for them, instituting internal controls to prevent their misuse or loss, and generally monitoring their proper use. In this role, Finance becomes something of a policing activity, making sure others don't damage the company through their actions.

- To organize all the data that it collects from company transactions and to present that data in a form that every-one in the company can use to more effectively manage their own functions and the company as a whole. In this sense, Finance provides information to help other depart-ments—its customers—do their jobs.

While these functions should generally carry equal impor-tance to the management of a company, they are not always carried out with equal enthusiasm by financial departments. In some companies, financial departments are more recognized for assertive policing than for serving the users of financial information. Policy constraints and procedural labyrinths seem to be the predominant preoccupation of these accountants, to the frustration of many outside the Finance Department. Yet, in other companies, the strong direction of operationally driven management can result in a financial department that is totally occupied with servicing a continuous flow of requirements for ad hoc information, at the expense of the protection function. In these companies, folks outside of Finance get their needs met, but auditors and others outside the company may be concerned about the safety of the company's assets and the efficient use of its resources.

In a perfect world, then, these functions would be balanced in a way that serves the best interests of the company's owners. A financial department that implements adequate internal con-trols and then enforces them with appropriate levels of enthusi-asm would have time and resources to serve the reasonable information needs of the enterprise as well. However, in reality, finding this balance is one of the most challenging management jobs in the company.

Manager's Checklist for Chapter 1

❏ Managers need to understand the rules of accounting and the boundaries of proper finance well enough to avoid getting into trouble as they aggressively try to achieve their goals.

❏ The financial department really has two fairly distinct jobs to perform in most companies: managing the company's financial resources ("Finance") and recording and reporting all its financial transactions ("Accounting").

❏ The standard format for recording and reporting financial transactions is outlined in guidelines, or rules, called *Generally Accepted Accounting Principles* (GAAP).

❏ One of the greatest challenges for management is to balance the two primary responsibilities of the financial department—to safeguard the assets of the company by properly accounting for them and monitoring their use and to organize information from transactions and present it so managers can function more effectively.

The *Structure* and Interrelationship of Financial Statements

E very corporation has, from the moment it is formed, an indefinite life under the law. The corporate laws of every state grant the right to perpetual existence to a corporation in order to enable management to take strategic actions that will have long-term impact on the company's survival and growth. These include the ability to make long-term contracts, the ability to issue certificates of ownership (stock) that don't expire, and so on.

As many have learned over the years, however, that is really only a legal definition. In reality, most companies follow a pattern of birth, rapid growth, slowing growth, plateau or no growth, decline, and demise.

Companies that react effectively to changes can minimize or even avoid the decline and escape the demise, but those are natural phases in the life cycle.

Unfortunately, the vast majority of new companies follow this pattern; eventually most close their doors. If you were even a moderate investor in the dot-com era of the '90s, you are likely able to rattle off a half dozen names that no longer exist

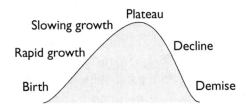

Figure 2-1. The life cycle of a company

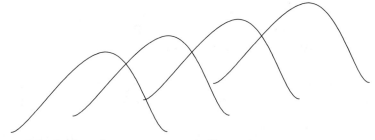

Figure 2-2. Prolonging a company's life cycle

(hopefully not because you owned them). Even outside the technology industry, there are companies that didn't have the right stuff to remain independent and they've fallen. Names that are rapidly fading into history include TWA and, more recently, Enron, Adelphia, and Worldcom.

As this is written, experts are predicting that 2002 will be the second record year in a row for corporate bankruptcy filings. Even if you allow that many of those filings were strategic moves to get relief from the demands of union contracts or loan agreements, it's still a matter of managers unable to live up to the commitments they once made in good faith.

Many more companies that didn't actually close their doors have been bought by other companies and, as a result, lost their separate existence, instead becoming merely a part of a larger, more successful company. You can still see names like Compaq, Time Warner, Texaco, RCA, and Chrysler. Yet none of these companies exists today as a stand-alone entity.

Yet the good companies continue to grow and seem to postpone indefinitely the time of their often-predicted demise through successive periods of renewal, rebirth, and resurgence.

Multiple examples of these can be found in names we recognize—IBM, Intel, and Apple Computer, to name a few.

Excellent companies, by contrast, seem to be forever resurgent, and while they occasionally pause in their progress, they never seem to actually go into decline. Examples that readily come to mind include General Electric, Southwest Airlines, Wal-Mart, and Microsoft.

A major difference among these companies, perhaps the overriding one, is their ability to react to change. Change impacts the ability of a company to capture and hold onto its market, to grow its business, to profitably sell its products, and ultimately to survive and prosper.

My 15-plus years of consulting experience tell me that the tendency of most business activity is to find those processes that seem to work and then repeat them over and over as long as they continue to function. This is considered efficient and among the proven techniques for maximizing profitability. However, every manager of a company, or a department, for that matter, must learn to differentiate between those business processes that must evolve, like research and development, and those that should remain stable. Financial accounting is one of those processes that need a high degree of stability.

Tracking the Life Cycle of a Company

As we have all learned in the past year or two, financial accounting probably needs more stability and less evolution than it has experienced, in order to give it adequate credibility in the eyes of the users of financial information. Managers rely on financial reports prepared from accounting data to guide their business decisions. Investors rely on those same reports to guide their investment decisions. Government relies on many of the same reports to collect taxes, enforce our laws, and protect investors, employees, and customers of those companies. Thus the recorders of financial data in a company carry a heavy responsibility to provide information that is, in a word, ARTistic—accurate, relevant, and timely.

ARTistic Financial Reports

Unlike the "creative" financial reporting we've seen from some major companies in the news in the past couple years, ARTistic reports are the cornerstone of sound reporting. The acronym means:

- **Accurate**—prepared with sufficient accuracy to be relied upon, without such a high accuracy requirement that they are too expensive or too time-consuming to produce. This concept in financial reporting is called *materiality*. (Generally, a matter may be judged material if the user of the financial reports would be likely to be influenced by knowing it. Materiality is usually considered in terms of the amount of money involved relative to the whole.)
- **Relevant**—presented in a way that is useful to those who must use them. A detailed listing of transactions with no totals or explanation might be accurate, but it is of little use to anyone and so not relevant for any business purpose.
- **Timely**—produced in time to be useful to those who need it. A totally accurate, relevant report that comes out three months late is not of much value because managers will have had to make decisions before it was available, in order to run their company.

While accounting rules may change over time to properly reflect changing business models and new types of business transactions, those changes must keep in mind the responsibility that accounting has to all its constituents—the responsibility to produce information that they can rely on. As we will see, that isn't always as easy as it sounds, but it is every bit as important as it sounds. That is why accounting as a business process needs to remain fairly stable, evolving only after very careful thought to the implications of reporting transactions differently than they might have been recorded previously. Remember that a major use of financial information is comparison with similar information from earlier periods to assess the degree of any changes. If the accounting methods are different, the conclusions may be flawed. As we have learned from the reports of executive shenanigans in recent years, it is far too easy to create incorrect conclusions if the rules allow too much flexibility.

In addition to stability, one of the key characteristics of the accounting process is repetition. The accounting process

achieves the highest degree of accuracy, relevance, and timeliness by use of its repetitive processes, enabling accountants to
process the most data at the least cost. The most common
repetitive process in the world of accounting is the monthly
closing cycle. A company goes through the traditional monthly
process of "closing the books" in order to see how the company
is doing in terms of its objectives, including profitability.

Accounting Is Like a Football Game on Videotape

Imagine yourself at home on a Saturday evening in November.
You're looking forward to watching the football game that was
played earlier in the day, while you were doing chores. You
recorded the entire game with your VCR and now you want to
watch it and really enjoy all the nuances of the action. In goes the
tape, you settle back into your easy chair, and you press Play.

In the very first big play of the game, the quarterback for
your team takes the snap, steps back, and deftly throws the ball
to a receiver 30 yards down the field. Just as the receiver reach-
es out to catch the ball, a defender's hands block him and prevent the catch. You're out of your seat in an instant, calling for
the referee to call "Interference" and penalize the defender. Then
you realize you can replay the action and see if there was any
illegal pushing. You stop the tape, go back to the moment of the
play, and freeze the action so you can study it in detail. Even
though the action didn't stop, your tape got every minute of it
and you can pick which segment of action to freeze for review.
Notice on the stopped tape that the ball is frozen in mid-air and
the players reaching for it are similarly frozen in time, feet high
off the ground. You can see exactly where everything was at that
moment—the players, the referee, and even the players in the
background who were part of the action elsewhere on the field.
In a real sense, it's a snapshot of a game moment, a photo of a
single instant in the 60 minutes of playing time.

Grudgingly satisfied that there was no interference, you
restart the tape. Your team marches down the field, nicely mix-
ing running and passing, until it has a first down on the visitors'

8-yard line. In a well-executed play, your team's running back takes the ball and charges through the pack, only to be tackled at the goal line. Did he get over or not? The referee says no. Once again, you stop the tape, rewind, and review. This time you're sure the ref is smoking something, because you have made your own analysis of the data and are convinced the score should now be 6-0 in favor of your team.

As you visualize this picture, keep in mind that the game was played earlier, before you got a chance to watch it, and it went on continuously for three hours (counting pileups, commercials, and halftime), despite your ability to stop the tape whenever you chose. The game didn't stop in reality, but your analysis tools enabled you to look back and analyze the action in as much depth as you wanted, because you had recorded with your VCR all the details of the game. In picture form that might look like Figure 2-3.

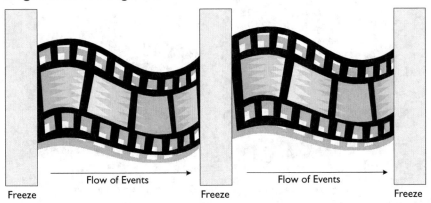

Figure 2-3. Flow of the action

As you can see, the action flows throughout the tape, but periodically your "freeze frame" commands to your remote resulted in an artificial stop in the action. When you press Play again, the action continues exactly where it left off, as if it had never stopped. Each vertical bar represents the freeze frame actions you took in an otherwise continuous flow of activity.

Now consider the financial transactions that occur every day in your company. Employees come to work, produce some sort of work result, and get paid. The company buys products and services, pays for them, adds its value to what it buys, and delivers a product or service to its customers. Then it bills them and collects its bills, enabling it to pay its bills in turn. This whole flow of activity is continuous every business day, all year long, for as many years as the company is in business. Yet once a month the finance department produces a report that starts promptly on the first day of each month and ends on the last day of that month. The accountants have found a way to stop the action for their purposes, even though it never stopped in reality, so they could report on the results for each period of "the game." They succeeded because they, too, recorded the action in their records. Think of the accounting books as an Accounting Transaction Recorder, or "ATR." Now we might change the labels in Figure 2-4 and see some similarities between the two recordings.

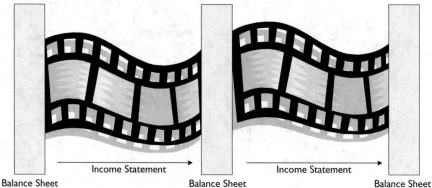

Figure 2-3. Flow of the financial action

As you can see, the "tape" starts when the business starts and the "freeze frame" status is captured in the company's balance sheet. Then there is a continuous flow of action, captured in the company's income statement and its statement of cash flow. The action never stops, but periodically, usually once a month, the accountants press the "freeze frame" button on their tapes, so they can analyze the progress the company made in detail. They then give you an income statement and statement of cash flow, adding up the changes that happened during the month-long activity, and a balance sheet, which shows where everything was on that last day of the month, when they pressed the "freeze frame" button. A quick look at the balance sheet shows you exactly where everything was at month end: how much the company was owed, how much cash it had in the bank, how much it owed to creditors at that exact moment, and lots more. In much the same sense as in the football game, the balance sheet is a snapshot of a single instant in the life of the company.

What's the big difference here? For the football game, you had to do your own analysis, using only your eyesight and your knowledge of the game of football. Of course, you can get extra value from hearing the announcers, particularly the ex-coach-turned-announcer, because they always describe things that their experience and keen eyes picked up that you didn't. The better you know the game, of course, the more useful information you can get from what they say, although the vast majority of listeners will miss most of the nuances.

In your company, by comparison, the accountants likely have in-depth experience and analytical tools to look at the data from different angles and they can prepare reports that tell you and others what the analysis reveals. Because you are always using the recording and replay device, the "ATR," you can study those reports at your leisure and even ask for clarification without losing a minute of company "game time." You could read the reports yourself without their help, but you

---

The Inside Edge

The more you know about the game of football, the more valuable insights you will get from the game reports, even though the vast majority of readers will miss most of the nuances. Not surprisingly, the analogy carries over. The more familiar you are with the concepts of accounting and finance, the more of the "hidden" information you'll get from your company's financial reports and the less time it will take you to get it, even though others may miss the point entirely.

probably couldn't produce the reports without their help, because you don't have an ATR.

The Chart of Accounts—A Collection of Buckets

If you've seen a chart of accounts, you probably wondered why the accountants hold this list in such high regard. You might hear phrases like "It's not in the chart of accounts. We don't know where to put it" or "We can't process your invoice without an account number." While to many non-financial managers, these phrases might seem intended primarily to retard the progress of commerce, that's not really their purpose—honest!

The entire recording process of any accounting system requires a basic organization of data so that the payment of vendor invoices, for example, can be later summarized and reported with some clarity as to what was done, why it was done, and what organization(s) benefited from those expenditures. That basic organization is called a *chart of accounts*.

You might think of the organizing system for your company's accounting data as a collection of buckets, or accounts, each with a particular kind of data inside. There might be a bucket for each individual asset the company owns and a bucket for each individual debt the company owes. There will also be a bucket for each product or service the company sells and one for each type of expense the company might incur as it sells its products or services. A company might have 200 or more buckets to hold all the transaction data about each of its assets and liabilities and each of its income and expense categories. Some companies might go a bit overboard in their desire to capture data ever more precisely. They might have ever-smaller buckets and sub-buckets to collect and sort data about the tiniest

Key Term

Chart of accounts A systematic listing of all ledger account names and associated numbers used by a company, arranged in the order in which they normally appear in financial statements—customarily Assets, Liabilities, Owners' Equity or Stockholders' Equity, Revenue, and Expenses.

kinds of income or expenses, in the interest of greater accuracy. It would be a challenging task to keep them straight if they were just lying around without any semblance of organization.

The chart of accounts is an organized, comprehensive list of all those buckets. The buckets, in turn, are labeled with their appropriate account number and arranged by the kind of data they hold, so that accountants can quickly find the right bucket in which to store the latest piece of data about a particular asset or liability. These buckets are then arranged and rearranged during the accounting process and their contents are counted and checked—usually monthly—to produce reports that summarize the data they contain.

Let's take a quick look at the abbreviated chart of accounts in Figure 2-5, to give you a quick idea what it might look like in a typical company. We'll discuss and define the major categories in the chart of accounts in Chapters 3 and 4, when we talk about the basic financial statements. After your quick look, you can forget what it looks like, as long as you remember its importance in categorizing raw accounting data into useful information.

Notice that there is a numbering convention used to help accountants identify assets from liabilities and income from expenses. There are endless schemes of account numbering,

Account Number	Account Description
	Assets
1000	Cash
1100	Short-term investments
1200	Accounts receivable—trade
1250	Allowance for uncollectible accounts
1500	Fixed assets
1510	Land and buildings
1520	Machinery and equipment
1600	Accumulated depreciation
1800	Deposits
1900	Long-term investments

Figure 2-5. Sample chart of accounts (continued on next page)

Account Number	Account Description
	Liabilities
2100	Accounts payable—trade
2200	Accrued payroll and benefits
2220	Accrued payroll
2230	Accrued payroll taxes
2300	Other accrued liabilities
2500	Contracts payable for leased equipment
2700	Long-term notes payable
	Stockholders' Equity
3100	Capital stock
3500	Retained earnings
3500	**Income**
4100	Sales of products
4110	Sales of Widgets
4300	Sales discounts and allowances
	Cost of Goods Sold
5100	Cost of manufacturing Widgets
5110	Direct Labor
5120	Materials
5600	Manufacturing overhead
5610	Factory rent
5620	Factory maintenance and repairs
5630	Factory insurance
	Operating Expenses
6000	Sales and Marketing expenses
6100	Salaries and wages
6120	Travel expenses
6130	Telephone
6200	Advertising
6300	Trade shows
7000	General and Administrative expenses
7100	Salaries and wages
7200	Insurance
7300	Postage and mailing
7400	Professional fees paid
	... and so on

Figure 2-5. Sample chart of accounts (continued)

but all will follow some similar kind of arrangement to facilitate the coding of transactions. Notice also that some accounts are indented and numbered to indicate they are subordinate to others. These sub-accounts provide a further breakdown of the larger categories into smaller categories to save time later in analyzing the data.

If you have spending authority in your company, you may be asked to approve invoices from vendors that you do business with. In some companies, that approval process could include assigning an account number to the invoice, to inform the accountants to whom the nature of the transaction might not be evident. In other companies, the issuance of a purchase order ensures that Accounting has all the information they need to process vendor invoices. If you are blessed to be in the latter group, you may never need to know anything more about the chart of accounts, except to know that it exists.

The General Ledger—Balancing the Buckets

You've probably heard the term *general ledger* and might even have joked that this must be the guy who secretly runs Accounting and issues all those reports no one can read. (Well, maybe not.) The original "general," as mentioned in Chapter 1, was a large post-bound book with large, ruled pages into which all the transactions of the company were carefully recorded by hand. It no longer looks like a book, except in rare cases. It's now likely to be a computer file, but it still carries the traditional name and it is still the place where all accounting transactions ultimately come to rest. It is also the data source for most of the basic financial statements that companies produce.

You might think of the general ledger as a large, old-fashioned scale that is always kept in balance because its keepers always add or subtract an equal and offsetting amount of weight to each side whenever they record something. All of the buckets that appear in the chart of accounts are arranged in one or the other of the trays, depending on the account number on the bucket (Figure 2-6).

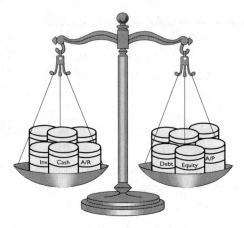

Figure 2-6. The balance sheet balances!

As each transaction occurs and is recognized, the accountants refer to the chart of accounts to find the name and location
of the correct bucket or buckets. Then they add to each bucket
the appropriate data that represents the financial effect of that
transaction. When they add something to a bucket on the Asset
side, such as a new delivery truck, they must finish the job in
one of two ways to rebalance the scale. Either they will take
away something of equal value from a bucket on the Asset side,

---

Surprise! The Balance Sheet Always Balances!

There is a relationship that is fundamental to financial
accounting: total assets must always equal the sum of total liabilities
and total stockholders' equity. Thus, if a company is able to conduct its
financial affairs in such a way that it can add assets without adding an
equal amount of liabilities, it has effectively increased the relative
weight of the company's ownership. Remember: the two sides must
always balance, according to the formula that is always true under the
rules of accounting:

Total Assets – Total Liabilities = Stockholders' Equity

Now, the insight that I hope will be immediately obvious is this: the
simplest way to increase assets without increasing liabilities by an
equal and offsetting amount is to make a profit.

such as the cash that was paid to the dealer to get the truck, or they will add something to a bucket on the Liability side, like the bank loan for the money that was borrowed to pay for the truck.

> **Stockholders' equity**
>
> The calculated amount of the total assets of a company that would theoretically remain if all the assets were sold off and all the liabilities paid off. It is typically composed of the total amount invested in the company by its owners plus the accumulated profits of the business since inception.

Thus the scale is still in balance and the company has a self-checking system to ensure the entire transaction has been recorded. Assuming the accountants have picked the right account buckets, the details of each transaction will be correctly captured and available for review at any time in the future. Codes attached to each piece of data enable the accountants to connect all the data pieces that were added to the scale as part of that particular entry, should the entire transaction need to be reconstructed in the future. For example, those various flags enable Accounting to know what was bought, from whom, for how much, on what date, and where it will appear in financial reports.

It is not a reflection of the actual amount that would be realized if the company were actually liquidated, however, because liquidation always produces actual net proceeds different from the amounts recorded for assets and liabilities. Thus, stockholders' equity is a guide, rather than an accurate measure of the owners' relative share of the business. Other terms that mean the same include *owners' equity* (often used for a sole proprietorship or partnership), *net worth*, *capital accounts*, *equity*, and *surplus* (not-for-profit organizations).

Accrual Accounting—Say What?

The accounting rules outlined in GAAP (Remember Chapter 1?) require that most companies keep their accounting records on the accrual basis. The alternative is the cash basis, meaning a transaction is recorded only when cash changes hands. Cash basis accounting is not considered indicative of economic realities, thus the requirement for accrual accounting except for certain kinds of companies, such as very small businesses and some not-for-profit organizations.

When the Sales Department obtains an order from one of your customers and the product is shipped to the customer, a sale has been consummated and it is recorded. This transaction will appear on the income statement even though not a single dollar may have passed from the customer to your company, because the customer has an open account with the company. The transaction is recorded by increasing Sales and by increasing Accounts Receivable, the amount due from your customer.

Later on, perhaps the following month, your customer pays his or her bill and your company receives the cash. That transaction will *not* appear on the income statement. It was already recorded as income when the sale was made and, under accrual accounting rules, only the sale itself is considered an income-producing event, not the act of collecting the money.

This example demonstrates the essence of accrual basis accounting. Transactions are recorded when an economic event is deemed to have occurred. A sale is an economic event because a binding agreement has been reached: your customer agreed to accept the merchandise and pay for it in due course and your company shipped the merchandise on your customer's promise to pay. That is an economic event, an offer made and accepted.

The customer's payment is another economic event. It is related to the first, but it is nevertheless a new event. The customer might have chosen to delay his or her payment or return the merchandise, but chose instead to pay for it. The second economic event doesn't affect Sales. However, it affects the balance in the customer's account and it increases your company's cash receipts. So when this transaction is recorded, Accounts Receivable and Cash are the accounts that are affected. This transaction, although not shown on the income statement, will be included in the statement of cash flow, which documents

> ## Don't Get Hung Up on Debits and Credits! ⚠️ CAUTION!
>
> In almost any discussion of accounting, you'll hear some-
> one talk about *debits* and *credits*. Those elusive terms that
> seem to exemplify the technical jargon of accounting are not, in my
> opinion, terribly useful for non-accountants. You don't really need to
> know that debits increase assets and decrease liabilities or that credits
> do the reverse. You only need to know the nature of the transactions
> that accomplish those things, and that has been well covered in this
> book. If you understand the idea of accrual accounting and the "buck-
> ets" discussed above, you won't need to worry about the debits and
> credits—unless you are applying for a job in Accounting, in which case
> this is the wrong book to be reading.

transactions other than those that affect income and expense.

Having tossed around the names of financial reports that we haven't yet defined, let's take a moment to do that and add the next piece to this puzzle called finance, before we move onto the next chapter.

The Principal Financial Statements Defined

There are three primary financial statement formats that appear in every annual report and most internal monthly financial reports as well. We mentioned them briefly during the football game analogy, but I want to reintroduce them here before we go into the next few chapters in which we'll discuss in excruciating detail their contents and appearance.

The Balance Sheet

This is the report showing the financial condition of the compa-ny as of a particular date, usually the end of a month, a quarter, or a year. It shows all the assets of the company, valued typical-ly at the cost to acquire them, but in some cases assets might be shown at the lower of cost or market value, when the accounting rules indicate a permanent reduction in value below cost. Similarly, the company's liabilities are shown at the amounts borrowed or owed. As you'll see, some of these are exact amounts, and some may be estimated based on the best

Balance sheet An itemized statement that summarizes the assets and the liabilities of a business as of a given date, usually the end of a month, a quarter, or a year.

available information. The difference between the carrying value of the assets and that of the liabilities is the equity interest accruing to the owners of the company. The balance sheet will be discussed in detail in Chapter 3.

The Income Statement

The income statement recaps all of the activities of a company intended to produce a profit. It shows the amount of sales, all the costs incurred in making those sales, and all the overhead costs incurred in running the operations of the company so it would be able to deliver on its promises to customers. This statement goes by various names, including *income statement, profit and loss (P&L) statement, statement of income and expenses, operating statement,* etc. In this book we'll call it the

Income statement An accounting of revenue, expenses, and profit for a given accounting period, usually a month, quarter, or a year.

Also known as income statement, profit and loss (P&L) statement, statement of income and expenses, and operating statement.

income statement, but keep in mind that your company may call it something different. All companies that keep their accounting records on the traditional accrual method produce a statement similar to this. The income statement will be discussed in Chapter 4.

Statement of Cash Flow

The income statement shows activities that were recorded with accrual basis accounting. However, companies that keep their books using accrual accounting still will have transactions that do not appear on the income statement, usually involving the exchange of cash. For example, your company borrows money from the bank and puts the money into its checking account for later use. No income created here and no

> **Statement of cash flow**
> A report that shows the effect of all transactions that involved or influenced cash, but didn't appear on the income statement. Also known as *cash flow statement*.

expense yet—until the interest begins to accumulate. So how do you get this on the books? And how do you report it? The answer is the statement of cash flow. It will show the effect of all transactions that involved or influenced cash, but didn't appear on the income statement. Going back to our football game analogy, you'll recall we noted about Figure 2-3 that these two statements between them would contain every transaction that occurs in a company between any two balance sheet dates. You'll learn more about the statement of cash flow in Chapter 6.

Other Report Formats

There are a wide variety of other reports that may accompany the basic statements in a financial report or be prepared separately for special purposes. They are often more valuable than the basic statements in managing specific areas of the company's finances. Examples include reports on accounts receivable, accounts payable, inventory, and much more. We don't have room in this book to cover all the possibilities, but we will mention some of them in later chapters as they relate to the subject.

Perhaps it is enough here to recognize that computerized accounting data today is increasingly maintained in flexible database formats that enable the accounting department to produce arrangements of data into a seemingly endless variety of formats. If you feel a critical need for information that you're not getting from reports now, a visit to the controller or the company bookkeeper might surprise you at how easily a responsive financial analyst can produce exactly what you need.

Manager's Checklist for Chapter 2

❏ Financial reports must be reasonably accurate, formatted in a relevant way, and delivered in timely fashion to be useful for helping managers make decisions about the company. For each ARTistic attribute, there is a trade-off between the degree of perfection and the cost of achieving it.

❏ The balance sheet is a snapshot of the financial condition of a company as of a point in time, while the income statement and the statement of cash flow tabulate all the transactions that have occurred during a period of time, i.e., between two balance sheet dates.

❏ The chart of accounts is an organized list of all the kinds of transactions that typically occur, so that transaction totals can be meaningfully grouped, summarized, and reported in financial statements.

❏ Accounting transactions are recorded in a balanced way, with each transaction affecting the scales equally, to ensure that the transaction has been recorded completely and correctly. If the scales are always in balance, the balance sheet will always be in balance.

❏ Assets always equal the sum of liabilities and equity. Put another way, assets minus liabilities always equal stockholders' equity or owners' equity. As a result, increasing assets without increasing liabilities by a like amount increases equity. This is achieved in its simplest form when the company makes a profit.

❏ The accrual method of accounting is the standard for nearly all companies. Under the accrual method, transactions are recorded when an economic event has occurred, such as a customer buying a product or the company purchasing supplies. The results of these transactions are recorded, in general, as soon as the commitment to enter into the transaction occurs, not when cash is received or paid for the commitment, which might be much later.

The Balance Sheet:
Basic Summary of Value and Ownership

In Chapter 1, we called the balance sheet a freeze frame, a photo, and a snapshot, to give you an idea of its purpose, which is to show the financial condition of the business at a single point in time. Now let's get away from the analogies and talk about what the balance sheet actually is and what it looks like.

Assets and Ownership—They Really Do Balance!

In this chapter we'll get into the nitty-gritty enough to help you understand the various line item labels that appear on a balance sheet, what they represent, and what you can learn from them.

Introducing The Wonder Widget Company

Let's build our discussion on an example. Throughout this book, we'll use an imaginary company, The Wonder Widget Company, a manufacturer of a wonderful new product for home and garden. Whenever we need an example, we'll call on our imaginary company's financial department to provide it. From time to time, we'll give you an actual example from our consulting files, but we'll adapt the example for The Wonder Widget Company.

ASSETS	
Current Assets	
Cash and Equivalents	$155,000
Accounts Receivable	940,000
Less Allowances for Bad Debts	(64,000)
	876,000
Inventory	
Raw Materials	311,000
Work in Process	65,000
Finished Goods	215,000
	591,000
Prepaid Expenses	45,000
Total Current Assets	$1,667,000
Fixed Assets	
Land and Buildings	1,250,000
Machinery and Equipment	750,000
Computers and Office Equipment	250,000
	2,250,000
Less Accumulated Depreciation	(972,000)
Total Fixed Assets	$1,278,000
Other Assets	
Deposits *(held by others)*	25,000
Long-Term Investments	276,000
Total Other Assets	$301,000
Total Assets	**$3,246,000**

Figure 3-1. The Wonder Widget Company balance sheet (Assets)

Let's call first for a *statement of financial condition,* more commonly called a *balance sheet.*

You notice that the two sides of the balance sheet—assets on the left and liabilities and stockholders' equity on the right— are in balance. That's nice. But what's actually shown on this magical balancing piece of paper?

LIABILITIES	
Current Liabilities	
Accounts Payable	$475,000
Accrued Payroll	57,000
Other Accrued Liabilities	31,000
Income Taxes Payable	54,000
Notes Payable to Banks, Short-Term	150,000
Current Portion of Long-Term Debt	52,000
Total Current Liabilities	819,000
Long-Term Liabilities	
Lease *(Purchase)* Contracts	125,000
Long-Term Debt *(other than leases)*	300,000
Loans from Stockholders	75,000
	500,000
Less Current Portion of Long-Term Debt	(52,000)
Total Long-Term Liabilities	448,000
Total Liabilities	1,267,000
Stockholders' Equity	
Capital Stock	50,000
Contributed Capital	1,750,000
Retained Earnings	179,000
Total Stockholders' Equity	1,979,000
Total Liablities	**$3,246,000**

Figure 3-1. The Wonder Widget Company balance sheet (Liabilities)

Let's look at each line item on our balance sheet and see if we can understand what they are and what they tell us about The Wonder Widget Company. (Our balance sheet has some italicized comments in parentheses, such as "*(held by others)*" next to the Deposits item under the Other Assets caption. These comments are to help you understand the line item; they would not normally appear on the page.)

Current Assets—Liquidity Makes Things Flow

Simply put, current assets are assets that are cash or are expected to become cash "currently," that is, within the next 12 months. These are the assets that produce most of the liquidity in a company and they are the main sources of working capital for the business. Here are the most typical examples of current assets.

> **Key Term**
>
> **Liquidity** The ability to meet current obligations with cash or other assets that can be quickly converted to cash, to pay the bills as they come due. In other words, the company has enough cash or enough assets that will become cash so that it is able to write checks without running out of money.
>
> **Insolvency** The opposite of *liquidity*, not having enough money to pay bills as they become due. Insolvency is often a precursor to a creditor revolt or even a bankruptcy filing.

Cash and Cash Equivalents

Cash itself is the most liquid asset of all and always the first item listed on any balance sheet. It includes Wonder Widget's petty cash fund, all the company's checking accounts, and cash reserves. Cash reserves might be kept in the form of savings accounts, bank certificates, money market accounts, short-term investments, and similar cash-like assets.

Companies vary in their policies about listing all the details of their various cash accounts: some will simply show "Cash" or "Cash in banks," while others will combine the details under a caption such as "Cash and short-term investments" or the more common caption used in our example, "Cash and cash equivalents." The important thing about all the items in this section is that they can be spent almost immediately, if needed.

Accounts Receivable

Amounts due from customers and others are usually next in the Current Assets section of the balance sheet. The largest of these is usually called accounts receivable; it typically means trade accounts or amounts due from customers as a result of sales

Long Collection Cycles by Intent

The toy industry is a good example of long collection periods. Toy stores sell most of their merchandise during the one or two months before the holidays. Yet toy manufacturers space their manufacturing activities over the entire year and then sell to their customers under special arrangements that allow the stores to pay for those purchases *after* they sell them, which mostly means after the holidays, perhaps many months after the goods were purchased and delivered to the stores. This practice is called *dating*, not in the boy-meets-girl sense but in the sense of extending the due date for payment. The sellers that engage in this practice must make sure they have enough cash or borrowing capacity to operate while they wait for payment.

made on credit. It's expected that customers will pay for those sales within a relatively short time (typically 30 to 60 days), so they are classified as "current," even though some customer accounts may actually be past due.

In some industries, business custom permits a much longer collection period, sometimes as long as six to nine months or even more. This practice enables makers of seasonal products to spread out their manufacturing over most of the year and induce their customers to take delivery of goods (but not pay for them) well before they'll be able to sell them, thus getting those inventories out of the makers' warehouses and into their customers' warehouses.

Also, during a recession it is not uncommon to find a company's customers experiencing cash flow problems that make it difficult for them to pay promptly. This might result in collection expectations that go beyond one year, although that will not usually be apparent from a glance at the balance sheet.

As a manager, you should remember that customers usually pay later than the terms your company may have granted them originally. The national average is estimated at about 45 days in normal economic times, longer than the customary 30-day terms printed on most invoices from their suppliers. So you can't always count on customers to pay their balances on time.

This is one of the key cash flow planning issues that companies face in managing their resources effectively. If Wonder Widget's customers don't pay promptly, the company will have less money to pay its suppliers, to order goods to replace those it has sold, and to pay its employees.

A typical balance sheet may show other amounts due the company than accounts receivable. They might include loans to employees or officers, tax refunds from the government, and other amounts due that are not strictly trade accounts with customers. In all cases, by classifying them as current assets, management is expressing the expectation that these amounts will be collected within a year.

Allowance for Bad Debts

Closely related to accounts receivable, but not always shown separately on the balance sheet, is an account called "Allowance for bad debts" or some similar title. This is a *reserve*, an estimated amount the company provides for the possibility that some customer balances will not be paid at all and will have to be written off. Any company that sells on credit has these kinds of issues to deal with—granting credit and managing customer relationships so that collection losses are as small as possible, consistent with good business practice.

Because companies cannot tell at first who will pay and who will not, they often provide a reserve for such losses at the time sales are made, typically calculated as a percentage of all sales made in a given period. Such reserves will then absorb the cost of bad debt losses that may be recognized in future periods.

In order to accomplish that, companies build reserves by creating a write-off to expense. They then charge uncollectible amounts off against the reserve whenever they decide they will not likely collect the full amount due. At any point in time, the allowance for bad debts is effectively a valuation adjustment account that reduces the total amount of customer accounts receivable on the books to the *net* amount expected to be collected.

Avoiding a Cash Management Pothole

TRICKS OF THE TRADE

Every company has to manage its accounts carefully to ensure they get paid in full and there are no bad debt losses. However, since periodic fluctuations in collection experience are a normal risk of doing business, smart managers who have this responsibility will arrange for credit lines with their banks in the event they cannot collect what is due them in time to meet their obligations to their creditors. A credit line is simply a promise by the bank to lend a company a certain amount of money to tide it over until its customers pay their bills. The company borrows however much it needs (within the credit limits) whenever it needs it and repays the bank when it collects from its customers. Interest is charged for only the time the amount borrowed is in the company's hands.

Inventory

Our next balance sheet item is inventory, a term used for production materials or products purchased or products manufactured and then held by the company for sale.

A company that manufactures its products might show several categories of inventory, like those on Wonder Widget's balance sheet:

- **Raw materials**—whatever the company uses in the manufacturing process, before it begins to change them into something else. It might be whole logs for a sawmill or it might be lumber for a company that makes furniture. The amount on the balance sheet is the cost of these materials, the amount paid to its suppliers to purchase them.
- **Work in process**—products in the midst of the manufacturing process, no longer raw materials but not yet finished goods. The balance sheet will include raw materials costs as well as some labor and related costs applied to these materials during the manufacturing process. You'll learn more about this process when we talk about cost accounting in Chapter 8.
- **Finished goods**—fully manufactured products ready for sale to customers. The balance sheet will show all the

> ## ⚠ CAUTION! ⚠
> ### Failing to Control Inventory Losses Can Cost a Bundle!
>
> Companies maintain inventories of their products so they can promptly satisfy customer demand for those products. The risk for any company is that it will keep inventory on hand that never sells or that sells only at a deep discount, for a variety of reasons, including the following:
>
> - It has more than its customers wanted (such as new cars at the end of the model year).
> - It stocked items that its customers didn't want to buy (such as marked-down fashion clothing at the end of the season).
> - The inventory became useless before anyone bought it (such as perishable food in the supermarket or a technology product that became obsolete as a result of a competitor's innovations).
> - Inventory was lost or was damaged or simply disappeared from theft or other causes and was not available to sell.
>
> When there are losses, inventory is revalued at a new, net realizable amount, and the difference becomes an expense on the company's books. Such expense can, if not properly controlled, become a large and unpleasant shock to a company's profit expectations. Companies typically examine and count their inventory periodically—at least annually or as often as monthly—in order to avoid unexpected losses in value.

costs needed to make the products, including labor and related overhead costs, such as factory rent, supervision, and product inspection.

By contrast, retailers, distributors, and trading companies usually purchase fully manufactured products, which they simply resell, without processing them any further. Their balance sheet will most likely show only a single line called inventory.

Prepaid Expenses

An unusual asset among current assets, prepaid expenses will never, except in rare cases, be turned into cash, in spite of our noting above that such conversion is a typical characteristic of current assets. Prepaid expenses are exactly that—expenses that have been paid in advance and therefore won't have to be paid again. Thus, in a sneaky way they create cash by enabling the company to avoid paying out that amount during the next 12 months. OK, so that's a stretch, but that's how it works—honest.

Let me give you an example. Every company buys insurance of various kinds and nearly every kind of insurance has a

> **Prepaid expenses**
> Amounts that are paid in advance to a vendor or creditor for goods and services. Because the payments are to obtain benefits for the organization over a period of time, the cost of these assets is charged against profits throughout the period, usually on a monthly basis. Prepaid expenses is a current asset, because the company has paid for something and someone owes it services or the goods.

premium that must be paid in advance, typically for a year at a time. Since insurance can be a costly item, companies want to allocate the cost of that protection over the period of time that is being protected. So, the company writes a check for 12 months of insurance protection and charges it to expense over the 12 months that it protects, usually by simply charging 1/12 of the total to expense each month. The balance of the advance premium payment is considered prepaid and it rests in a prepaid expense account until it has been entirely written off to expense. Other examples of prepaid expenses might be property taxes or income tax installments.

Fixed Assets—Property and Possessions

Every company acquires physical assets that it uses to conduct its business—computers, manufacturing equipment, buildings, land, trucks, and so forth. Those assets are used for extended periods of time, usually years, and are thus not current assets in the sense of the items discussed above. These are usually called "Fixed Assets" or "Property, Plant, and Equipment" or perhaps—if no real estate or vehicles are owned—"Equipment and Furnishings."

Since such assets are used for a number of years and are not held for resale to customers, they are not considered sources of liquidity or cash flow. They are, well, "fixed" in place, until they are no longer useful to the business. At that point, they are either sold or discarded and then replaced.

Fixed assets may not move around much, but during their period of use, their value declines substantially, often to zero by the end of their service. The sole exception to this is land, which does not decline in value, but is more likely to increase in value over time. In order to recognize that reduction in value, a company will depreciate, or systematically write down, the cost of each fixed asset (except land, which almost never declines in value) over the period of time that it will be used in the business.

That reduction in value is charged to expense when recognized, under "Depreciation Expense" in the income statement (see Chapter 4). On the balance sheet, the total amount written off to expense since a fixed asset was purchased is shown under "Accumulated Depreciation." This account is shown immediately after the original cost of fixed assets as a deduction from original cost, so that the net value of fixed assets is readily apparent to anyone who reads the statement.

Avoid Getting Caught with Your Assets Down!

Smart Managing In evaluating a company, look carefully at the relationship between fixed assets and accumulated depreciation shown on the balance sheet. If the accumulated depreciation is a large percentage of total fixed assets and very little remains to be written off, it may be a sign that the company is facing potentially heavy expenditures in the near future to replace aging equipment that may no longer be able to do its job. In an industry influenced by technology, such as automobile manufacturing, this may be even more of a concern. Alternatively, keeping old equipment in place may result in higher maintenance and repair costs. Either way, it could be a clue to future drains on cash flow or the need to borrow money for replacement purchases.

The smart strategy: keep up maintenance programs on equipment with long service lives, to avoid shortening useful lives unnecessarily. When equipment must be replaced, use return on investment (ROI) calculations to find the best way to finance the replacement.

Other Assets—The "Everything Else" Category

At the bottom of the Assets side on most balance sheets is a catchall category called, cleverly, "Other Assets." These are holdings of the company that are neither current nor fixed. Assets in this category are not expected to become cash in the next 12 months and they are not real estate, machines, or equipment used in the operation of the company's business. They may not even be directly related to the company's business.

For example, a deposit paid to a landlord from whom the company leases its offices would be found here, since most such leases are multi-year commitments. Remember: a lease deposit is not really a current expense to the company, because it can be either applied against final rent under the lease or returned to the tenant when the property is vacated. So a rent deposit may be disbursed at the beginning of the lease but not become expense until the end of the lease, if at all.

An investment in another company will be listed here as well. Wonder Widget apparently has made at least one such investment. By putting this item in the non-current category, it is saying it intends to hold this investment for an extended period of time. In other words, it's not a readily marketable security that is going to be sold as soon as the price goes up a few points.

Current Liabilities—Repayment Is Key

The Liabilities side of the balance sheet also begins with what's current. Once again, liquidity is the measure of the label "current," but in the case of liabilities it is *negative* liquidity—cash going *out* the door. Current liabilities are all those debts of the company that are expected to be paid within the next 12 months, the same period in which the current assets are expected to become cash.

The relationship here becomes evident if you think about it for a moment. Current assets will become cash to pay off current liabilities. That is the principle of working capital in any company. If you look at Wonder Widget's balance sheet (Figure

> **Key Term**
>
> **Working capital** A common but theoretical way to measure the amount of ready liquidity of a company. To calculate it, deduct current assets from current liabilities. Also called *net working capital*. For example, Wonder Widget's current assets total $1,667,000 and its current liabilities total $819,000. Thus it has net working capital of $848,000.

3-1), you'll notice that current assets are about twice current liabilities, usually thought of as a pretty good relationship to ensure that the cash will be available when needed. You'll read more about that relationship in Chapter 7, when we discuss critical performance factors.

Accounts Payable

This is the account that includes all the bills yet unpaid from all the suppliers and service providers. This is usually the largest item among a company's current liabilities. Accounts payable is usually the first item listed under current liabilities.

Amounts in this category should be paid in accordance with trade terms printed on the invoices, typically 30 days, or whatever other payment period was granted by the supplier. Sometimes companies take longer to pay their bills than the official period, as noted above for accounts receivable. In such cases, customers are, in essence, borrowing money from their trade creditors to help increase the amount of financial resources that are at work in their company. This is called *leverage*, and we'll bring this up again in Chapter 5 and in discussing ratios in Chapter 7. When Wonder Widget extends its payment period by delaying payments to its creditors, it's benefiting from the use

> **Key Term**
>
> **Leverage** The ability to put more money into a business than has been invested by its owners and thus earn more than its invested capital could earn alone.

of leverage. When its customers do the same thing to it, Wonder Widget's accounts receivable take longer to collect and it's on the wrong side of that leverage.

Often a company will show other amounts it owes under separate labels in order to make sure readers of the report know that there are amounts due for these "special" liabilities. Wonder Widget's balance sheet shows income taxes payable as such a category.

Accrued Payroll

Next on Wonder Widget's statement of financial condition—remember that alternative name for a balance sheet—is this account, which represents the amount earned by employees but not yet paid to them. Since employees are typically paid for time already worked, not in advance, every company has some amount of compensation

---

Delay Can Pay

If a company can earn 12% annually by buying and reselling merchandise, it can earn almost 1/4% on every dollar that it can delay paying its creditors by a week. A company with an average balance of $50,000 in accounts payable could earn about $115 a week or $6,000 a year. Of course, it may not be worth it if the company incurs additional charges or jeopardizes its standing with creditors.

The Cash Squeeze—Don't Get Caught in the Middle!

Keep this thought in mind: despite all the headlines around bank lending practices, venture capital investing, public offerings of stock, etc., the largest single source of operating capital for most businesses is the money they borrow from their creditors, that is, accounts payable. Almost every entrepreneur has a few stories about the struggles he or she went through to squeeze more working capital out of his or her balance sheet. This usually means increasing available cash by delaying payment to creditors, while at the same time trying to make sure their customers don't do the same thing to them.

Sometimes the squeeze play goes against you. The company can't collect its accounts receivable on a timely basis, and its creditors won't let it slow down its payments. The result can be a disastrous cash flow crunch! Companies in the construction industry often face this. Their customers hold up payment for unfinished loose ends on a project, while their subcontractors insist on being paid to prevent mechanic's liens from being placed on the property.

earned by its employees but not yet paid to them. When a company keeps its accounting records on the accrual basis (refer to Chapter 5 for a discussion of accounting methods), such liabilities are recorded when they become owed, even though they don't actually have to be paid until later on. The only exception would be those companies that pay employees on the last day of their workweek, in which case at the end of a payday they would not owe any money to their employees—until the following day.

Other Accrued Liabilities

In the same fashion that Wonder Widget records its payroll earned but not yet paid, a company will usually have other such liabilities as well. These may be expenses the company has incurred, but for which it has not yet received an invoice to record. In order to make sure the expense gets recorded into the right accounting period, the company's accountants will accrue the liability rather than wait for an invoice to arrive or a check to be issued. Examples might include large purchases for which the supplier has not yet invoiced the company or interest expense on a loan that doesn't get invoiced, but for which the bank will automatically charge the company.

Notes Payable and Other Bank Debt

Loans from banks and others that represent borrowed money and not simply trade accounts with suppliers are always shown separately because the loans and the repayments typically have special terms. When you see notes payable to anyone, particularly banking institutions, you can be pretty sure the company has agreed to some kind of limitation on its range of activity, called *covenants*, as a way of ensuring the ultimate repayment of the loan.

While borrowing to finance the business will be discussed in Chapter 10, you should keep in mind that when such loans appear on the balance sheet, you can expect to see other kinds of guarantees provided to the lender, such as pledging assets as collateral, a personal guarantee of repayment by the owners of

> **Loan covenant** Clauses in a loan agreement that require the borrower to do certain things ("affirmative covenants") and/or not do others ("negative covenants") during the term of the loan agreement. Some typical covenants include the following:
> - The company must maintain adequate insurance.
> - The company must furnish financial statements quarterly and annually.
> - The company cannot allow other liens on company assets.
> - The company cannot merge with another company or acquire another company.
>
> Banks will often monitor compliance with loan covenants quarterly, based on the financial statements, and sometimes require that a corporate officer or independent accountant issue a compliance certificate that serves as evidence that no covenant violation has occurred.

the company, or perhaps even a contingent claim on the ownership of the company.

Current Portion of Long-Term Debt

Refer to the discussion below of long-term debt. This "current" caption simply represents the portion of that debt that must be repaid within the next 12 months.

Long-Term Liabilities—Borrowed Capital

You might see a wide variety of long-term borrowings on a company's balance sheet, including the line items seen in Figure 3-1. Rather than try to describe all the items you might find listed under "Long-Term Liabilities," let's just look for a moment at the types seen on our sample balance sheet.

Lease Contracts

This label shows commitments made by a company in order to lease equipment or other assets at favorable payment terms, usually followed with a modest payment buyout option at the end. According to U.S. accounting rules, when a lease contract is designed primarily to finance the intended purchase of the asset, the asset and the liability are recorded on the lessee's books and accounted for as if the asset had actually been purchased with a loan agreement instead of a lease contract. Remember: a lease can also be simply a long-term rental agreement in which there is no actual transfer of ownership, and therefore no recording of the asset and liability on the company's books. However, some leases are written more like purchase agreements than leases, which is why they often appear on balance sheets, as in our example.

Long-Term Debt

A company with financing needs that extend out for years might opt to borrow money with a payment term that extends out as far as possible, enabling it to put the money to use and earn enough to easily repay the loan. In such cases, entire amount of the loan is reported as a long-term debt and the portion of that loan that is due to be paid within the next 12 months—meaning "currently due"—is shown under "Current Liabilities." This is what Wonder Widget has done in our example.

Loans from Stockholders

This is another special category of loan, most often seen on the balance sheets of privately owned companies operated by the owners. For some privately owned companies, this is how owners put money into the company when it needs it and take it back out again when it doesn't. All too frequently, however, business conditions may not improve soon, so loans from stockholders may stay on the balance sheet for years. In fact, banks and other outside lenders may actually require that such balances remain unpaid as long as the company has outside loans. Thus, these amounts can end up looking more like owners' equity than loans to the company, often a frustrating reality for entrepreneurs and small business owners, who had hoped to be repaid at some point.

Ownership Comes in Various Forms

Owners' equity or stockholders' equity (for a corporation) or capital (for a proprietorship or partnership) is the owners' stake in the business. It includes what they have invested to launch, to finance, or to refinance the company and what the company has earned over its existence.

As noted above, it can also include amounts that owners have loaned to the business that they cannot get back because of some subsequent loan agreement with a bank or other lending source. Such loans are always shown in the liabilities section of the balance sheet and never in the equity section, because they are not legally investment capital until and unless ultimate repayment is formally relinquished by legal means. Captions that may appear in this section include the following.

Capital Stock and Contributed Capital

Capital stock is the amount paid into the company by investors to purchase stock, at some nominal amount per share. It is usually a small part of what the investors actually paid, for legal reasons that you don't even want to hear about. Let's just say that investors usually pay more for a share of stock than the amount shown under this caption; the balance of the proceeds is reported under a heading such as "Contributed Capital" or some similar description. These two amounts, when combined, represent the total amount formally contributed by investors to finance the company.

Capital stock The amount paid into the company by investors to purchase stock, at some nominal amount per share, the par value printed on each share of stock. Par value is an arbitrary dollar amount assigned to shares of stock for accounting purposes during the incorporation process, usually set as low as possible in order to minimize legal restrictions on the amount classified as par value. Many corporations today assign no par value to their shares to avoid this problem entirely.

Additional contributed capital or additional paid-in capital The amount paid into the company by investors to purchase stock, beyond the par value of the stock. Also sometimes a general label used to include both capital stock and additional paid-in capital, especially when capital stock has been issued at no par value.

Retained Earnings

Every company, from its inception, develops a history of profits and losses. Profits add to retained earnings and losses reduce retained earnings. If a company has operated with overall profitability, it will have accumulated a substantial amount of earnings over time. If it is a proprietorship (unincorporated, one owner) or a partnership (unincorporated, two or more owners), these earnings are usually taxable to the owner(s) immediately, so they are typically paid out to the owner(s) each year, as dividends or distributions of profits.

> **Key Term**
>
> **Retained earnings** Profits of a business that have not been paid out to the owners or stockholders (as dividends) as of the balance sheet date. These earnings are reinvested in the business.

However, if the company is a corporation, its owners will not generally be taxed on the company's accumulated profits until the company chooses to distribute those earnings to its owners in the form of cash dividends. In the interim, the accumulated earnings not distributed to its owners are shown as, logically enough, retained earnings.

Earnings are retained in the business for other reasons than just to avoid paying taxes on them, including enabling the business to retain cash for expansion or to purchase land, buildings, and equipment (fixed assets) to facilitate its operations. The company may also be building a "war chest" to enable it to:

- Buy other companies
- Protect itself against a possible catastrophe
- Repurchase its own stock, when prices are low
- Ensure adequate working capital to run the business

Wonder Widget is a relatively new company, so its retained earnings are still low.

Some companies actually have negative retained earnings, because they've lost more money than they've made over their existence. (This is the situation for most airlines.) You can usually recognize this by the caption "Deficit in retained earnings."

This is usually a good clue that you might not want to buy their stock just yet, as they may not yet have figured out how to make money in their business. (This was a story heard frequently in recent years in the aftermath of the dot-com collapse of 2000-2001.)

Using This Report Effectively

The balance sheet is the status report of the company's financial health. It shows where the company is strong, such as good cash balances and low amounts of debt, and it shows where the company is weak, such as large amounts of debt classified as "current," minimal retained earnings, etc.

Often the answers it provides are your cue to ask the question "Why?" It is a good idea to be familiar enough with the balance sheet to be able to know which questions to ask.

Pay particular attention to the ratios and analysis tools that we'll discuss in Chapters 7 and 9 for some excellent ways to get more information in less time when looking at a balance sheet.

Manager's Checklist for Chapter 3

❏ The balance sheet is the report of the company's financial condition at a certain moment. It will provide valuable information about the success of the company's cash management practices, its history of profitability, and the adequacy of its invested capital. Often the most valuable information it provides is simply showing the right questions to ask.

❏ *Current assets* and *current liabilities* are closely related. Current assets are very liquid and should be able to be converted into cash within a 12-month period. Current liabilities, in turn, must be repaid with that same 12-month period, usually from the cash raised out of the conversion of current assets. The difference between the two is called *net working capital.*

❏ A large amount of accounts receivable may look good on the balance sheet, but their collectibility is the most important issue, and that's not always apparent by simply looking at the total. Look at "Allowance for bad debts" and the customer-by-customer details to better understand the true quality of this balance.

❏ Inventory represents a constant management challenge and a relatively high-risk area for losses unless inventory management practices are solid. There are lots of ways inventory can cost a company money, including deterioration, obsolescence, and breakage.

❏ Accounts payable is the largest source of day-to-day financing for most companies. Delaying payment can provide temporary relief for cash-strapped companies, thus causing accounts receivable collection problems for their creditors.

The Flow of Profits and Cash

The Income Statement: The Flow of Progress

L et's go back for a moment to our football game analogy. You'll remember we identified the income statement as a report that tallies the cumulative effect of all the income and expense transactions that occurred between two balance sheet dates. All those transactions typically are conducted with the idea of producing a profit for the company. The income statement shows the company's success in achieving that objective.

They Say Timing Is Everything—And They're Right!

The income statement is the report that most non-financial managers readily recognize. They know it shows whether the business made a profit for the month, the quarter, or the year. In large companies and small ones, managers' bonuses are often based on profit results (too often, even though they have little control over the profit—but that's another subject). Others see it as the report most valued by their CEOs, shareholders, bankers, and government regulators. Some managers recognize it by its format, but are used to calling it a different name, such as profit and loss (P&L) statement, statement of income and expenses, and a few others.

Whatever you call it, it's usually acknowledged to be the most important report a company produces. (But hold your vote until you've read Chapter 6.) As such, it behooves us to spend a little time understanding how it comes together, and why that matters.

While non-financial people readily recognize the importance of the income statement, they don't always appreciate how transaction timing affects profit in any given period. In fact, they're often surprised that monthly reports don't show the effects of individual transactions that they reasonably expected to see, even though nothing has been missed or been reported incorrectly. There are two culprits in this plot:

- The passage of time between the date a transaction was first committed to a supplier or a customer and—through the processes of fulfillment, invoicing or billing, and recording—the date payment was made or received.
- The confusion that sometimes arises over when a transaction should properly be recorded, under the accounting rules. (Remember GAAP from Chapter 1?)

Regarding the first culprit, time, there's often a long sequence of events that must be completed before a transaction may be recorded. The final step of a transaction can be recorded days or even weeks after the initiating department has finished its role in the process, e.g., filling the customer's order. It might be even longer before the transaction is complete, e.g., the company collects from the customer.

As for the second culprit, confusion, I can recall one typical incident when I was the controller for a large company with a nationwide sales organization. A regional sales manager with budget responsibilities questioned a financial report that showed expenditures charged to his department in June, when he had made the deal with the supplier to provide the merchandise or services in April. "Why wasn't it taken out of my budget in April when I spent the money?" he asked.

The Widget Isn't Sold—or Recorded— Until It Works

Imagine the new salesperson on the staff of Wonder Widget selling an advanced version of the Wonder Widget, the Enterprise Widget. The salesperson does a great job of selling the product's benefits and tells the customer the price includes full installation and training, with no commitment to pay until it works. So, the customer signs the order. The paperwork goes into Wonder Widget's sales office for processing and the salesperson enthusiastically goes on to the next deal, hoping for a commission check before sunset. Meanwhile, the process of setting up the customer begins, including credit application, credit checking, shipping instructions, etc. Then the product finally ships to the customer. Done, right? Nope. Actually, it's just beginning.

This Enterprise Widget isn't "plug and play" like its predecessors; it requires installation, setup, debugging, and finally training, all of which are part of the product package. By the time all that is completed, months have passed and the salesperson still has that sale on an open item list—"I sold it but they haven't yet paid me for it." Yet the company can't hold the customer to the sale until the installed product is accepted. Under the rules of accounting, when the customer is irrevocably committed *and* the company has delivered on its promises, the transaction can be recorded. Under Wonder Widget's commission plan, the commission is payable under the same circumstances. So, no sale, no commission.

Expenses do not get recorded when they are committed, when the order is called in, when a purchase order is issued, or even when the supplier agrees to supply the goods or services ordered. All those things are simply requests or promises, all of which can be rescinded without penalty. So they're not the irrevocable transactions that we can record. When the supplier acts on that promise to deliver, then we have an accounting event that should be recorded and the money is really spent.

Why would the sales manager even care about such refinements of accounting? Well, first, he was being evaluated on his performance against budget, of course, always a good tool for instilling budget consciousness. But mostly he wanted to be relieved of the need to keep track of money he had committed and (in his mind) spent. It's easy to understand his desire, since keeping track of such details is time-consuming. If the money were charged against his budget when it was committed, he would know how much he had left to commit or spend in later months.

The questions made sense to the sales manager, yet frustrated the accountants. They could never quite convince him they had done it right, especially since they sometimes hadn't. Yet the best answer lay in better communication between the two groups about how accounting works.

Today, many companies have integrated enterprise accounting systems that can keep track of purchase orders issued but not yet fulfilled, and it's much easier to track and report commitments made for future goods and services. Even so, such commitments cannot be booked as actual expenses until the goods have been delivered and the purchase order satisfied. This is the flip side of the sales example above, but the same accounting rules apply.

With that overview in mind, let's look at the line items in a typical income statement. As an example, let's use the most recent income statement of The Wonder Widget Company. Take a look at Figure 4-1, and then read on.

Sales: The Grease for the Engine

"Nothing happens until you sell something." This is the sale to customers of products and services *that the company regularly*

Smart Managing

If It Counts Toward My Bonus, It Must Be Sales

A good example of conflicting objectives that can cause misunderstanding is the answer to the question, When is it sold? The corporate scandals reported in the press during the past couple years included equipment service contracts that one company recorded as equipment sales. Why? Probably because equipment sales go into profit immediately, while service contracts can be recorded only as the service is rendered, often over months or years. A sale recorded now counts for more than a sale that will be recorded next year, especially if you're watching earnings per share this quarter. A smart manager understands about conflicting objectives and the dangers that result.

Sales		$650,000
Cost of Sales		475,000
Gross Profit		175,000
Operating Expenses		
Engineering	25,000	
Sales and Marketing	76,000	
General and Administrative	37,000	138,000
Operating Income		37,000
Other Income and Expenses		(5,000)
Income Before Expenses		32,000
	24,000	
Income Taxes		12,800
Net Income		19,200
Earnings per Share		$0.10
Fully Diluted Earnings per Share		$0.08

Figure 4-1. The Wonder Widget income statement

offers for sale in the normal course of business. This means we don't include the sale of surplus equipment off the shop floor, because that's not our business. We also don't include the sale of a building that we're not using anymore (unless our business is buying and selling buildings). It also means, as noted above, a sale that has been completed, an irrevocable transaction for which the customer is required to pay.

Depending on your business, *sales* might be called different things on your income statement. Sales of services are often called *revenue*, although the terms mean pretty much the same thing, and there are no real differences in the rules between sales of products and sales of services. We will use the terms interchangeably in this book.

Cost of Sales: What It Takes to Earn the Sale

The cost of sales is, logically, the costs directly related to delivering on the sale. It always includes the cost to make or buy the

> **Tricks That Tempt Managers into Trouble**
> When the outside world looks so intently at a company's sales for clues as to its success, it's sometimes hard
> for some companies to resist the temptation to cut corners in the
> interest of making their shareholders and potential shareholders smile.
> Because some of the accounting rules seem to have room for inter-
> pretation, occasionally they get interpreted all the way into the next
> room. Here are some examples that you will want to look out for:
> - Recording sales too soon, before the transaction is complete, e.g.,
>   such as when the quarter is ending and the CFO wants the compa-
>   ny to look good.
> - Recording sales too late, e.g., waiting until the next month or quar-
>   ter because your CFO doesn't expect that quarter to look as good
>   as this one, and he wants to even them out a bit.
> - Recording sales that haven't really happened (yet), but that the CFO
>   is sure will happen momentarily, and so why not slip them in a bit
>   early?

product or service sold, including the cost of delivering the merchandise or components to the selling company. It should also
include the costs of other services that were packaged and sold
along with the product, such as installation and training (if they
were a part of the sale). Finally, it might also include directly
related selling expenses, such as costs of delivery to the customer and sales commissions paid to salespeople, although this
is not a universal practice. This may also carry the label cost of
goods sold, if selling expenses are shown elsewhere.

Gross Profit: The First Measure of Profitability

This is a key measure of profitability, one we'll talk about in
more depth in Chapters 7 and 8. Gross profit is the gain the
company earns after selling its products and paying for all elements of the cost of sales. Earning a gross profit is very important, because the difference between sales and the cost of sales
normally pays all of the operating expenses discussed below. In
other words, if you sell each widget at a loss, it's highly unlikely
you will make it up the loss through volume.

Start with the inventory on hand at the beginning of the month, valued at the total actual cost to make or buy it.	$175,000
Add the cost of all the inventory purchased during the month, which was intended to be used in making the company's products, either now or later.	275,000
Add the cost of the labor used to manufacture products during the month.	215,000
Add in the other costs incurred by the company indirectly related to making its products, such as plant electricity, machine depreciation, supervisory salaries, and so on.	415,000
This is the total cost invested in inventory for sale during the month.	1,080,000
Deduct the total cost of inventory still remaining unsold at the end of the month.	(210,000)
The difference is the total cost of goods sold during the month or the cost of manufacturing the goods sold.	870,000
Add the costs incurred to get the products to the customer, such as delivery freight, commissions, etc.	30,000
This is the cost of sales for the month.	$900,000

Figure 4-2. Cost of sales—a sample calculation for a manufacturing company

Operating Expenses: Running the Business

This category includes all the operating costs of the business, what it takes to keep the doors open and to support the sales of the company's products. Usually there are subcategories shown on the income statement, as we've done in Figure 4-1, to show the operating expenses for each of the major functional activities of the company.

These are typically the following:

- engineering or research and development
- sales and marketing
- general and administrative expenses

There can be other categories of costs, depending on the nature of the company's business. For example, a drug company might carry separate categories for research and for product development, because these are such significant cost areas for a company in that business. A distribution company that buys and sells products made by others would have no reason to have research or development costs, but it might have a large category called Distribution Expenses, because that's a significant area of expense for a distribution company.

Let's look briefly at what each of these categories of expenses typically includes.

Research and Development: Finding Something New!

Research and development (R&D) is money spent to create new products or to significantly improve existing products. The classic example is the drug company that spends millions in the laboratories exploring diseases for which there's no cure known, in the hopes of making an exciting discovery that will pay off for all its research spending. It doesn't always work out that way, of course, and most R&D expenditures are ultimately unproductive in terms of developing a product that can be sold. Still, a company that depends on a flow of new products to survive in the marketplace must allocate a portion of its spending each year to research if it is to stay in business.

Closely related are groupings of expenses often called *engineering expenses*. Some companies prefer this caption, perhaps because they do not think of themselves as engaged in basic research, but rather in using engineering methodology to improve on what's already known about their business.

Further down the line from basic research and engineering is an area called *product development*. This is the cost to take the fruits of that research and produce new products that can be sold, e.g., a cure for the common cold in simple pill form. It can also be intended to improve existing products, such as a better nasal spray or even a better dispenser for the same nasal spray.

These are all costs that a company incurs to find something new to sell. A company that can afford to spend more for R&D has a better chance of staying ahead of its competitors. Having better products sooner than others should provide an edge, at least for a while. As you can see, a company will be motivated to allocate as much of its resources as possible to R&D in the belief that it will pay off in sales. R&D is a cost the company incurs before it will have the opportunity to make a sale and then, as it's making sales, to ensure that sales will continue. In other words, R&D is a cost of doing business that must be financed out of the gross profit.

Sales and Marketing Expenses: Positioning the Company to Sell Something

We noted earlier that direct costs of making a sale, such as commissions for salespeople, are often reported as a part of the cost of sales. Beyond those costs directly related to making a sale, substantial effort and cost goes into creating and maintaining a sales and marketing presence.

Marketing costs are all those expenditures a company makes to find out what people want to buy from it, to interest people in its products, and to create prospects for the company's sales force. Typically, none of these costs are directly related to making a sale, yet they're necessary to create a steady flow of prospective buyers for the salespeople. Market research, brand development, and test marketing are all examples of marketing costs.

Selling expenses, by comparison, are the costs of actually selling the company's products and services. This includes putting salespeople in the field to call on prospects and get orders or on the telephone to take orders. It includes distributing sales brochures, advertising, trade shows, and all the support costs of the sales organization. Sales and marketing, then, is another cost of doing business.

General and Administrative Expense: Running the Back Office and Paying the Rent

The third common category of expense is *general and administrative expense* (G&A). This is sort of the "all other" category, because it includes everything not grouped under some other heading. If it's not production, research, development, engineering, sales, or marketing, then it must be G&A. Examples include the costs of executive salaries, accounting and human resources personnel, many corporate and employee welfare costs, and all the costs of supporting the company's administrative organization. Yep, another cost of doing business.

Operating Income: The Basic Business Bottom Line

The next important measure of overall profitability, operating income is the profit that comes from doing what the company is in business to do. This key number is not yet the "bottom line" we so often refer to, but it's close. More importantly, it's usually the final result of the company's *normal* business activities, before unusual, nonrecurring, or financially related items that are often considered incidental to what the company is in business to do.

For Example

Selling a Company Is Not Operating Income

During 2002 IBM was criticized for selling a small subsidiary company at a profit and recording the profit in its income statement under *general and administrative expenses* (G&A). Putting that profit into its G&A effectively reduced the G&A expense reported for that year. This is a desirable thing for stockholders to see in a report, because it implies that a presumably ongoing expense has been reduced. In fact, this was a one-time-only item, ongoing G&A had not been reduced, and some stockholders and media reporters felt misled by the presentation. IBM said the profit was so small it was immaterial. But the idea still stuck in the minds of investors and the media, probably because it was seen as still another example of loose financial reporting by public companies, an issue exploding on the news scene at the time.

EBITDA—He Bit Who?

Nowhere to be seen on Wonder Widget's income statement is the term seen so often on reports issued by a growing number of companies in recent years, *earnings before interest, taxes, depreciation, and amortization.* Folks who fancy buzzwords will appreciate the buzzword for this one—EBITDA, pronounced "ee-bit-dah." Duh.

EBITDA is a modified way of presenting operating income for organizations that are not concerned about the financially oriented charges that it excludes. Consider a profit center within a company—perhaps a division whose job is simply to produce operating income. The division general manager is relieved of concern for corporate office decisions about how to finance the business (remove interest expense), how long to depreciate its assets (remove depreciation and amortization expense), and how to pay or defer its taxes (remove income taxes). The resulting calculation is closer to a pure operating income at the unit level, probably where this measurement got its initial support.

> **Key Term**
>
> **Earnings before interest, taxes, depreciation, and amortization (EBITDA)** A financial measure for evaluating a company often used as an approximation of operating cash flow. Also sometimes known as *operating profit before depreciation.*

Later on, of course, it began appearing on published income statements of companies with heavy investments in equipment and heavy debt loads, as a way to show their earnings without the burden of these financial charges. Its relevance will be judged over time, but for our purposes, just think of it as a different version of operating income.

But let's get back to what our income statement actually shows.

Other Income and Expenses—Not Just Odds and Ends

Finally, there are the nonoperating items, such as interest

expense on borrowed money and profits or losses on selling nonbusiness assets that are likely to happen in the normal course of doing business, but are not part of running the business.

Typical examples include:

- Interest income and interest expense, considered financial costs and not operating costs (unless your company is an insurance company or a bank, for which the rules are different)
- Gain or loss on selling off equipment no longer used by the company
- Gain or loss on the disposition of investments that were incidental to the business.

These items are shown near the bottom of the income statement so that they don't detract from the reader's conclusions about how well the normal business of the company is going. While typically small in relation to the operations of the business, they are not necessarily minor. In fact, some of them can become very large in relation to net income, especially if the company's profit margins are modest. An example might be the sale of unused land the company has held for many years, often at a price many times greater than the value at which it was carried on the company's books. When such items get very large, they will most likely be labeled *extraordinary items* and shown separately, sometimes even with a separate calculation of earnings per share to show their impact on the bottom line.

Income Before Taxes, Income Taxes, and Net Income

We're coming to the bottom of the page now, and we have now arrived at a number often called *pretax income*. The formal label you will most often see is *income before taxes*, although there are variations of that as well, for reasons that even I don't understand. In any event, they all mean the same thing—the income that the company expects to pay tax on, the amount on

> ### Pretax Income and Provision for Income Taxes Are Usually Wrong!
>
> Oh, OK, not wrong because they were calculated incorrectly, but because they're rarely the actual amounts reported on the company's tax returns. They're estimates, and often not even based on the tax returns actually filed, but on a complex calculation that blends GAAP and the tax laws. So take these numbers with a grain of salt and don't expect to see them on the company's tax returns. No matter, though, because the difference isn't usually controllable, and the number you really want is the last one, net income.

which its income tax estimate is based. Immediately following that is the income tax estimate, usually called *provision for income taxes* or something like that.

The number that matters most comes last, *net income*. This is the *real bottom line*. It's the final financial result of everything the company has done for the period being reported, after all the reasons, the excuses, the bragging, and the complaining. This is it—the final act, the last number you'll every see. Well, almost.

Earnings per Share, Before and After Dilution—What?

For a privately owned company and its principals, nothing matters after Net Income. But if your company is publicly traded and the financial statement is one of the quarterly or annual reports that are issued to the media, what seems to matter more than net income is a little thing called *net income* per share of stock owned by stockholders, better known as *earnings per share* (EPS).

In this little calculation, net income is divided by the number of shares held by all the owners. The result is the amount of that net income (or loss) that is allocable to each share of stock. This is a powerful number in the hands of a media representative, an investment advisor, or an investment banker touting an upcoming stock offering. Why so much attention? It's the easiest way an individual who owns 100 shares of

General Motors stock can tell how his or her ownership participated in the company's huge earnings, just as effectively as the investor who owns 100,000 shares of GM. And all those reporters and advisors have made EPS one of the principal gauges of a company's profit performance, and thereby one of the principal indicators of the stock's possible price performance.

The only problem is that there's no one number for EPS, with the result that many companies routinely report two such numbers: earnings per share and *earnings per share fully diluted*. Huh? Why two? Well, it seems that some company employees—and perhaps others—are holding options to buy some of

Dilution Can Be Hazardous to Your Investment

Let's suppose you bought 10,000 shares of XYZ stock and there are 100 million shares outstanding (including yours). Now, suppose the company reports net income of $100 million for last year. A little quick arithmetic and we can figure out that's $1 per share of earnings for each of those 100 million shares outstanding. Now let's suppose that the *price/earnings ratio* is 20. That would make the likely value of each of your shares $20 and your investment would be worth $200,000. If you bought the stock for $18, you now have a $20,000 profit (on paper).

But wait! There are some stock option holders out there, who could purchase 5 million shares of XYZ stock. They like the earnings report as much as you do, so they all exercise their options right after the report. Now there are 105 million shares outstanding, to divide up that $100 million in income, so each share now has claim on only 95 cents of earnings, not $1. At the same P/E ratio of 20, your shares are now worth $19 each, not $20. Because of the dilution, your profit drops from $20,000 to $10,000—a drop of 50%.

that stock, and they may be just waiting for the right time. In the interim, they represent the possibility that there will be more people dividing up that net income than there are now. That is called *dilution.*

As the "For Example" sidebar shows, dilution can significantly affect earnings per share. So, the accounting rules say you must be able to easily see the effects on EPS if all those option holders exercised their options. Fully diluted earnings per share is almost always shown under the regular (primary) EPS on a public company's income statement. That way you can see what your smaller share of earnings would be, worst case, and make your investment decisions accordingly.

> **Price/earnings ratio** The relationship between a stock's price and its earnings per share, calculated by dividing the price per share by earnings per share for a 12-month period. For example, a stock selling for $50 a share and earning $5 a share has a P/E ratio of 10. The ratio—the most common measure of how expensive a stock is—gives investors a rough idea of how much they're paying for earning power. Also known as *earnings multiple, P/E multiple,* or *multiple.*

Using This Report Effectively

The income statement is a very useful tool for understanding a company's performance in a very high-level way. Internal income statements used by company managers are typically more useful than those generated for outsiders, because they contain details that are not in the highly summarized versions that are published. The best way to use an income statement is to put it alongside income statements for prior periods or against the expectations of the company ("the budget") or against income statements of other companies similar in nature. It's by comparison against some benchmark that the income statement has its greatest value. It's by comparison that you can assign a grade for performance that's not possible when looking at just a statement for a single period.

Manager's Checklist for Chapter 4

❏ Don't get confused by the wide variety of line item labels on income statements. The labels are attempts to adapt to top management preferences or unique aspects of one company or industry compared with others. Look for the common thread, e.g., marketing is marketing, even if the label is a little different.

❏ Don't get tempted by accounting tricks. Remember that sales belong in the periods in which they were earned and completed, not necessarily where they look good.

❏ There are a few really key numbers on any income statement: sales, gross profit, operating income or EBITDA, and net income. These are the numbers that are most often used to measure profit performance by everyone who has an interest in the company.

❏ The income statement is the most familiar measure of a company's performance over a period of time. Its value increases substantially if it's compared with a benchmark, such as a budget, prior month, or prior year. The comparison enables you to better judge the company's performance.

Profit vs. Cash Flow:
What's the Difference—and Who Cares?

M any participants in our workshops are surprised to learn that instant profits and rapid growth aren't always cause for celebration. I tell them the story of The Wonder Widget Company.

The startup company launched with $100,000 in cash and the hottest product in its market, the amazing Wonder Widget. The owners had sales and profits from the first month they had a product to sell! All they had to do was make the product and ship it to waiting customers who would pay enough to give Wonder Widget handsome margins from day 1. And so they leased and outfitted a factory (no cash outlay initially), leased the production equipment and furnishings (still no initial cash outlay), bought the materials, hired the workers, made the product, and shipped it. They then mailed invoices totaling $50,000 to customers in their first month of sales. Amazing!

They paid their bills as they came due and collected from customers in the normal course of doing business. Their customers were sometimes a bit slow, of course, but nothing out of the ordinary, the kind of 40- to 50-day payment patterns that most companies see today. And sales continued to grow, increasing by $50,000 every month, with no decline in margins and no serious competition. Profits climbed without a pause. The owners didn't have to build much of an inventory, because everyone wanted the same single product, so they just made them and shipped them as fast as they could. This was a business your mother would love!

Yet a strange thing happened on the way to the bank. The owners were suddenly shocked to find that they didn't have enough cash to pay their bills. They soon found they couldn't buy more materials to make more Widgets, then they couldn't make payroll, and finally creditors went to court and nearly had the company closed down. Instantly profitable Wonder Widget was insolvent six months after they opened the doors!

Now, I hope you would ask, how could that happen? Good question. Let's try to answer it.

To do that, we need to look at how cash typically flows through a company. We'll again use Wonder Widget as our example.

The Cash Flow Cycle

At the beginning of the cash cycle, nearly every business starts with—you guessed it!—cash. But from that point on, the central purpose of the business is to convert that cash into other kinds of assets, to leverage or extend it with liabilities, and to ultimately turn it back into cash again, but *more* cash than the business started with. This process continues indefinitely and simultaneously throughout the entire existence of a business.

Cash cycle In general, the time between cash disbursement and cash collection. In manufacturing, this cycle would consist of converting cash into raw materials, raw materials into finished goods, finished goods into receivables, and receivables back into cash. Also known as *cash flow cycle*, *cash conversion cycle*, and *operating cycle*.

In the final analysis, then, when a company closes its doors, the only real financial measure of its success is the difference between the amount of cash it started with and the amount it ended with, after considering cash distributed to its owners over the life of the business. However, during the life of a company, we can't very well judge how much cash it would produce if it closed and liquidated, so we must measure success in terms of how it succeeds in conducting activities that will ultimately produce cash, usually measured in terms of profits and other financial factors included in the monthly reports we discussed in Chapters 3 and 4.

Let's look at this cycle as it applied to Wonder Widget by referring to the diagram (Figure 5-1), in which activities are moving clockwise in an endless process as the business operates.

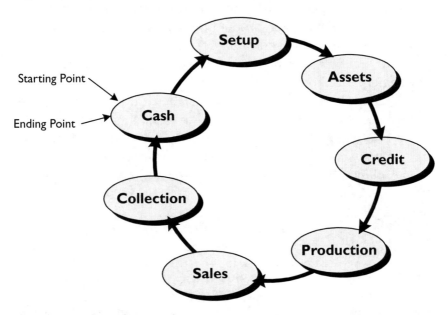

Figure 5-1. Cash flow cycle

When Wonder Widget started up, its first activities revolved around *setup*—renting facilities, getting phones and utilities installed, and the like. Most of this required the outlay of cash for rent deposits, phone equipment, utility deposits, and a variety of related costs.

Closely related to the setup, and often happening simultaneously, is the purchase of *assets* to commence business operations. These include office equipment and computers for administrative purposes and factory equipment to begin manufacturing widgets. For distributors, wholesalers, or retailers, those costs would include equipping warehouse space in order to stock the merchandise that that they will buy and resell.

The most important asset for any business is people, of course, and Wonder Widget was probably hiring staff all along the way toward the start of production—to answer phones, to run the office, and to produce and sell their product. Of course, this can get pretty expensive. If the owners had lots of cash, they might have paid for all these things by simply writing a check. Usually, however, prudent owners will choose to go to their bank or a finance company of some kind to get an extended period of time to pay for their larger purchases, such as machinery, furniture, and buildings.

That is where the company takes the next step in the cycle, obtaining *credit*. The main purpose of credit in a growing business is to enable the owners to increase the amount of capital they have working for them by using creditors' capital in addition to their own. This is called *leverage*, putting more capital to work for the business, as discussed in Chapter 3.

There's Profit in Borrowing

Borrowing money enables you to increase the capital that you can put to work for you. For example, if you have $1,000 and you can invest it and earn 10%, you'll make $100 a year in profit. However, if you can borrow $4,000 more from a bank at 5% interest, you can now put $5,000 to work earning 10%, which will produce $500 a year. Your net profit, after paying $200 interest, will be $300, much more than if you'd invested only your $1,000. You've leveraged your $1,000 and tripled its productivity. (You'll read more about leverage in Chapter 7, Critical Performance Factors: Finding the "Hidden" Information.)

In any event, cash is still going out at this point, even though credit may allow some delay in payouts. We know the Wonder Widget owners used credit to leverage their cash, because unhappy creditors later took them to court.

Wonder Widget was now ready to begin *production*, manufacturing Widgets. They began using their inventories of materials, adding the labor of the workers they have hired and a host of other costs needed to complete their product. This process consumed even more cash—workers' wages and related taxes, materials to replace those consumed in production, sales and marketing efforts to find new customers for their products, delivery of products to customers, billing, administration and accounting, and so on. This is typically the period of greatest cash consumption, when a company is in full production but no cash is coming in yet. The company hasn't sold anything yet or has sold products but on credit, so the customers haven't paid yet. At the same time, production and all the related business activities mentioned above must continue.

Continuing on with the remaining steps in the cash flow cycle, the company finally, after investing all that cash, gets to actually sell something and begin the process of recovering that cash it's been investing. In the *sales* part of the cycle, it succeeds in selling products, on credit of course, and sends out invoices that say "Net 30" on them. That means the customers will pay them 30 days after the date on the invoice, right? Not likely.

While *collection* may seem like a minor activity compared with production or sales, it's the critical step needed to make all the rest pay off. Nolan Bushnell, founder of Atari and Chuck E. Cheese Restaurants, has told his employees and countless audiences of would-be entrepreneurs that *a sale is a gift to the customer until the money is in the bank*. So, the final step in the cycle is the one that turns the entire effort back into cash again. At that point some key answers will surface: Did the company ultimately make a profit on its business activities? Did the company plan adequately for the working capital it will need to finance the cash flow cycle in its entirety? As we've seen in the

Wonder Widget example, one "yes" out of two isn't enough.

Now, let's stop for a moment and consider the situation. The owners of Wonder Widget had a hit on their hands in terms of demand. There were lots of people eager to buy their new widgets and the company probably pushed productivity to the limit to meet as much of that demand as possible. So they ordered lots of materials, hired lots of laborers, shipped lots of product, and then waited for lots of customers to pay them.

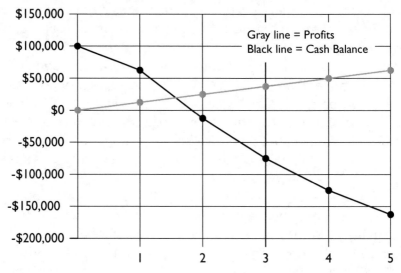

Figure 5-2. Cash flow curve of a fast-growing startup company

They had to invest their cash up front to set up the company, make the product, ship the product, and invoice the customers. Meantime, since a new company often doesn't get much slack from its vendors, they probably had to pay their bills on time, often earlier than if they'd been in business for a while. And of course, if their customers thought that startup Wonder Widget was glad for the business and would be patient for their money, some may have delayed slightly in paying their bills.

But none of these things by themselves would have rendered the company insolvent, yet the sum of them did exactly that, because they all added up to critically delay the cash flow.

Fast Growth Means a Big Appetite for Cash

Smart Managing

Fast-growing companies need more working capital than those growing more slowly or not at all. When incoming cash flow is delayed while fixed costs continue and paydays come every week, there's a limit to how long a company can operate comfortably, even if profitable.

Managers in fast-growing businesses should follow these three rules:

1. Look for every opportunity to stretch their cash, especially for large purchases.
2. Forecast their cash needs as far into the future as they can reasonably see.
3. Arrange added sources of cash well before they might need it.

Now you may look at our little company, Wonder Widget, and say that the owners could have done something to help themselves, in spite of their failure to use some key management tools. For example:

- They could have raised their prices to produce more profit sooner. And that would have helped eventually, but perhaps not in time. In fact, they were very profitable from the beginning. The problem wasn't in making a profit, but in converting that profit into cash in the bank.
- They could have gotten accounts receivable financing to help them get cash out of their receivables sooner. This might have helped too, and perhaps it was part of the ultimate solution. But history shows that most lenders aren't willing to lend to new companies until they've proven able to conduct business reliably, so that customers are less likely to raise complaints that would prevent prompt collection of the accounts used as collateral for the loan.
- They could have raised more capital for their business from friends, family, or outside investors. We don't know if they tried this and were unsuccessful because their urgent need made potential investors wary, but we do know they didn't raise money in time to prevent the cash flow crisis.

But that's not the point of the story, is it? The managers of Wonder Widget had made a serious management error, in spite of the great product, seemingly endless demand, and super profit margins. And it could have cost them their company. First, they didn't forecast their expected cash flow needs during their critical early months, a subject that will be discussed in some depth in Chapter 10, The Annual Budget: Financing Your Plans. Second, they didn't recognize the need to track cash flow results separately from profits. They looked at an income statement each month, saw that their efforts had produced a profit, and happily moved on.

> **CAUTION!**
>
> ## Business Goes with the Flow
>
> The health of a business depends on a healthy cash flow. More businesses fail because of a lack of cash than because of a lack of profits. Cash flow is not profits; it's all a question of timing. It's essential, then, that cash flow be properly understood and managed as carefully as revenue, expenses, and profits.

So if cash flow is so important, why doesn't it show up in the books somewhere? Or if it does, how can we make it easier to understand? Well, it really does show up in the books, since every transaction involving cash is recorded somewhere. The challenge comes in putting it into a format that's easier to understand. (We'll discuss the statement of cash flow in Chapter 6.)

Cash Basis vs. Accrual Basis

As it turns out, financial reports can look quite different depending on the accounting method you use to keep your books. There are two basic choices of accounting method, as discussed briefly in Chapter 2—*cash* and *accrual*.

The reality of small business is that many companies keep their books on the cash basis because it's simpler to understand—sort of like running the business out of your checkbook—and because it often coincides with the way they file their tax returns. And as long as you don't care about the strict definition of profits, that can work. An example might be a con-

> **Cash basis accounting** A method of accounting in which
> financial transactions are recorded only when cash is
> involved. Similar to keeping a checkbook, a sale is recorded
> only when the cash is received, and an expense is recorded only when
> a check is written to pay for it.
>
> **Accrual basis accounting** The more common method of accounting
> in which financial transactions are recorded when they actually happen,
> even if the payment is made later. A sale on credit is recorded when the
> customer is invoiced, and a purchase on credit is recorded when the
> goods are received, even if the supplier's bill is paid much later.

sultant who sells her time to clients. She's not very concerned
about gross margins, because her operating costs are relatively
low. But she's very concerned about cash flow, because without
it there's no paycheck for her.

On the other side, far more small businesses (and all large
ones) keep their books on the accrual basis, usually for one or
more of three reasons:

- They're concerned about gross margin on products they
  sell.
- They want to really know when they're making money
  and when they're not.
- They're required by lenders, investors, or government
  authorities to report their activities that way.

These are all good reasons to use accrual basis accounting,
and most experts would commend that choice. But many of
these same companies look only at their income statements
and often don't even prepare cash flow reports. Instead they
rely on good old rule-of-thumb methods to manage the cash so
that they don't run short or let unused cash sit idle.

Our purpose here is not to tell you which accounting
method is best for you—although like most professionals we
prefer accrual accounting because it gives most business owners so much more useful information. Rather, we want to help
you understand the differences between accounting methods so
you can make the better choice. But regardless of which

method you use, you'll keep in mind the importance of looking at the other method in some fashion, so you can get the benefit of the management information that awaits you there.

So let's take a closer look at some of the things that Wonder Widget management overlooked. In the process, you might see how your own company's team might use its financial reports more effectively. For the sake of clarity, we're going to assume that your records are kept on the accrual basis of accounting, reflecting transactions when they actually happen, as discussed in Chapters 3 and 4.

Net Profit vs. Net Cash Flow in Your Financial Reports

So, how does bottom-line profit differ from cash flow, exactly? Or, more specifically, how do individual transactions affect your company's reported profits and cash flow differently? Anyone who has compared income statements and bank statements knows that profit never makes its way to the bank account in exactly the same amount that appeared on the income statements. That difference is primarily the result of four kinds of transactions that we'll examine in the following paragraphs:

- Transactions that increase profits but don't produce cash until later
- Transactions that decrease profits but don't reduce cash until later
- Transactions that put cash in the bank first but don't help your profits until later—if at all
- Transactions that take cash but may or may not affect profits later

Let's look at each of these in turn.

Type 1. Transactions That Increase Profits but Don't Produce Cash Until Later

This is perhaps the largest and most obvious example of the difference we are talking about—and the most significant item in this group is *accounts receivable*. Consider the following example.

If your business is a retail store, you typically sell something and get paid in cash. The result is an increase in sales and a corresponding increase in cash in the drawer. But if you're a supplier to that retailer—the wholesaler—you'll typically wait anywhere from 30 to 120 days or more to get paid, depending on the industry and the time of year. You still record a sale when you ship your merchandise, but you don't receive payment at the same time. You issue an invoice with the payment terms of the sale, typically 30 days or longer. The retailer records the invoice into accounts payable when the merchandise is received and pays it weeks or months later, ideally in accordance with its terms. In the interim, you must accept the fact that although you have a sale and a resulting profit, you have no money to back it up. You must plan, then, to have enough cash on hand or instantly available to pay operating expenses between the time you ship the merchandise and the time your customer pays the invoice, often including the cost of the merchandise itself.

For companies that sell on credit, waiting for customers to pay their bills is the largest single factor necessitating extra cash availability.

Type 2. Transactions That Decrease Profits but Don't Reduce Cash Until Later

The other side of the coin is the situation that produces an expense or profit reduction first and a cash disbursement later. The most obvious example is accounts payable, liabilities that you incur when you purchase consumable supplies and services on credit. The supplies and services are typically charged to expense (profits) when purchased, although the supplier's bill might not be paid until the following month.

Let's take our Wonder Widget example. The owners might have gained some cash flow advantage from purchasing their raw materials on credit, as most businesses do. In fact, given the demand for their products, they might have even put some of those raw materials into production before they had to pay for them. If they did, they could potentially have shipped fin-

> **Key Term**
>
> **Cost of goods sold (COGS or CGS)** A common varia-
> tion on the cost of sales concept discussed in Chapter 4,
> cost of goods sold represents all the costs of manufacturing
> or buying the products sold during the month, including raw materials,
> manufacturing labor, and related overhead costs, but excluding the
> directly related selling costs that are a part of cost of sales. Figure 4-2,
> which you saw earlier, showed how the two terms differ in their calcu-
> lation. Depending on which approach a company takes, its gross profit
> and gross margin percentage will be slightly different, although operat-
> ing profit will be the same in either case.
>
> Companies that purchase and resell goods rather than manufactur-
> ing the products they sell will for the most part report the cost of
> purchased goods on this line rather than accumulating raw materials
> and direct labor.
>
> To add to the terminology collection, companies that sell services
> rather than products will usually report this line as cost of services
> rather than cost of sales. This subtle distinction has lost ground in
> recent years as some service companies have dispensed with the term
> altogether, opting instead to simply report revenues, operating expens-
> es, and operating profit.

ished goods to customers before they had even paid their suppliers for the raw materials that went into the product. They
would have recorded as expenses the costs of those goods,
commonly called *cost of goods sold* (see Chapter 4), even
though they had not yet written a check to pay for the materials. This would have postponed paying, but not delayed recording costs in their income statement. Thus, costs would appear
on their income statement even though no cash had left their
bank account.

Type 3. Transactions That Put Cash in the Bank but Don't Help Your Profits Until Later—if at All

Cash flow means everything that affects your bank balance.
That includes sources of cash that might never impact profits.
Consider the effect of going to the bank to borrow money. You
get the loan, put the money into your bank account, and thus
experience positive cash flow. Yet there is no change in your

profits as a result of the loan—aside from the good things you might do with the money later that *will* improve profits. But you don't get to keep the money forever; sooner or later you have to repay it. That comes up in the next section.

Closely related, particularly for new companies, is the effect of having outsiders invest in their company. The investors write a check and the company banks the check and issues stock to its new investors. The company can use that money, but it will never appear in the income statement. Wonder Widget started operations with money like that, and it was recorded directly on the balance sheet as capital stock, not in the income statement as sales of stock.

Type 4. Transactions That Take Cash but May or May Not Affect Profits Later

Do you remember the loan that puts cash in the bank without recording a profit increase? Well, the repayment of that loan is the flip side—money is paid out but there's no reduction in profits. Of course, while you have the loan outstanding, you'll have to record and pay interest on it, which is recorded as interest expense on your income statement. But the principal reduction portion of your payment is simply returning the money to the bank, a transaction that affects both sides of your balance sheet but not your income statement.

Another example of a cash payment with a delayed impact on profit is the purchase of assets for a business—machinery, automobiles, etc.—that will typically benefit the company for a number of years. A manufacturing company might buy the production equipment by paying cash for equipment that might last five or 10 years or more. Because the assets are purchased to benefit the business for years to come, accounting standards require that the cost of those assets be charged to income over the periods that received the benefit, not the month in which the assets were purchased and paid for.

Of course, a manufacturer might choose to finance its purchases through installment contracts or leases and thus bring its

Depreciation The amount of expense that a company charges against earnings to write off the cost of a capital asset over the time it will benefit the company, without regard to how it was paid for and after coinsidering age, wear, obsolescence, and salvage value.

There are various methods of calculating this expense, most originating from favorable tax laws. If the expense is assumed to be incurred equally over the life of the asset, the method of depreciation is *straight line*. If the expense is assumed to be incurred in decreasing amounts over the life of the asset, the method is *accelerated*. The straight line method is more common: the total cost of the asset is divided by the number of months it will be used and the result is charged to expense each month until the asset is retired or sold off.

cash payments and the periods benefited more into alignment. It might finance a machine over five years and depreciate it over the same five years. For many assets, this is helpful but doesn't solve the problem entirely, as financing periods are often shorter than the useful lives of the assets being financed, e.g., a factory machine might last seven to 10 years or more, yet few banks will finance such purchases for longer than three to five years. Thus, even in this seemingly ideal scenario, you will still have a disparity between the cash disbursement and the recording of depreciation expense.

Another example is the area of prepaid expenses (discussed in Chapter 3), which are amortized. An example might be an insurance policy on which an annual premium is paid in advance. When you buy insurance and pay the premium, that policy provides protection for a year. Proper accounting treatment says that the premium benefits all 12 months and should therefore be charged to profits over the benefit period, not just the month in which you paid the premium. So, you write your check in January 2003, but you record as expense only 1/12 of the check amount each month during the next 12 months, the period of coverage. Cash flow and expense are reflected totally differently in this example.

As you can see, some of these examples describe transactions in which the cash flow will never affect profits, but most are cases where the expense and the cash flow happen at different times. Business managers often overlook these timing differences because they "know" the effects will

> **Amortization** The process of spreading the cost of an intangible asset, such as research and development expenditures, over its expected useful life. Intangible assets are amortized in the same way as tangible assets are depreciated.

pretty much equal each other over time. But they forget how significant such differences can be in the short term, when the most critical cash flow planning is done.

Manager's Checklist for Chapter 5

❑ Cash flows throughout every company in an endless process that converts cash to operating assets and expenditures and ultimately back to cash again. The secret is to manage the process so that there's more cash at the end than at the beginning. The management challenge is to know how well you're succeeding at that when a company is operating normally, with many cash cycles occurring at the same time.

❑ Net cash flow is never the same as net profit; managers must track both to be well informed about the financial condition of their company. The best way to do that is to ensure that monthly financial reports are prepared that show both measures—cash flow and net profit.

❑ Managers in fast-growing companies always need more working capital to support growth. They should consider every opportunity to conserve cash for future growth by such means as financing large purchases and arranging backup lines of credit before they're needed.

❑ Businesses routinely take on obligations that require large amounts of cash, such as building inventories and extending credit to customers. Much of that investment is a necessary cost of doing business; however, keep in mind that every dollar invested in inventories and accounts receivable is at risk of loss before it again becomes cash.

❑ A forecast of estimated cash flow six to 12 months into the future is an excellent tool for management. It gives managers time to make decisions and arrange alternative sources that can prevent surprise cash shortages.

The Cash Flow Statement: Tracking the King

We've examined the income statement in some detail in the preceding chapters. We've noted its importance in measuring the performance of an organization, and its familiarity as the financial statement most readily recognized and understood by nonfinancial folks. We should also note its shortcomings as the sole report card on financial operations, perhaps most importantly:

- It doesn't report on all the transactions that occur in a company unless they have an immediate impact on profit or loss. Many transactions without such immediate profit and loss impact can be for big dollars, such as buying new equipment for the plant or borrowing money from the bank.
- It doesn't explain why the net profit on the income statement never appears as an actual improvement to the company's bank balance.
- It doesn't give growing companies a tool to manage their most scarce resource, cash to finance growth.

For that reason we suggested in Chapter 4 that you resist voting for the income statement as the most important single financial report until you hear from the unheralded, often unseen, and frequently unread, but resoundingly relevant *statement of cash flow.*

Most everyone has heard that cute phrase: "Cash is king!" Yet for many business professionals, that most often means making sure there's money in the bank or in the cash register or in their pockets. However, if there's one thing that consulting professionals, lenders, and turnaround experts all agree on, it's that the cash a company has on hand is a *trailing indicator* of its financial condition. In other words, by the time the status of a company's liquidity is reflected in the bank account, the cause of the problem is already history and there's not much managers can do about it. They will often focus on the symptom, fixing the cash shortage, instead of finding and fixing the original cause of the problem—product pricing, operating efficiency, credit granting policy, or a host of other possible causes.

So, the trick for every manager is to be regularly aware of where the cash is coming from and where it is going, both for historical evaluation and for future planning purposes. How best to do that? Well, there are two choices: they can pore over their cash journals and bank statements and prepare an exhaustive analysis of their bank account transactions each month *or* they can prepare an automated financial report that summarizes those transactions and identifies the general causes of increases and decreases. Hmmmm …. Which one should we choose?

Well, just for the heck of it, why don't we go with the financial report? And just to make our job easier, why don't we pick one that actually shows us all the major reasons net profit didn't produce an identical amount of cash going into the bank? Huh? There couldn't be a single report that contains that much information about something as critical as cash or it would be on the desk of every manager who has any kind of financial responsibility in his or her company, wouldn't it?

Ladies and gentlemen, allow me to introduce to you the statement of cash flow.

OK, maybe that's a bit dramatic. But the reality isn't that far afield from my playful musings. Most small businesses, for example, don't prepare a statement of cash flow as a routine part of their monthly financial reporting, even though almost all accounting software systems produce one. In larger companies with well-staffed accounting departments, the report is often produced, but infrequently read, except by the accountants and the CFO, whose job it is to act on it (and perhaps tell others what it says).

Beginning Where the Income Statement Ends

There are two or three formats for presenting the cash flow statement; in this book we'll use the *indirect method* of presentation. It's the same format as appears in all published financial reports of public companies and the same format as the report that's readily produced by most accounting software. It's also the format that produces the most useful information with the least paper. And the really good news is that it begins where the income statement ends, literally, because its intent is to answer that important question raised earlier, "What is the difference between net profit and net cash flow?"

Answering that question gets us into defining the differences and then presenting them in a way that non-financial readers can understand. A few words about format will be helpful here, before we actually look at a report.

Accountants have presented cash flow in two ways traditionally, the *direct* method and the *indirect* method.

The direct method is likely what you might prepare if you were analyzing your checking account to see where the money came from and where it went. It would look something like Figure 6-1.

As you can see, the report shows cash coming in and cash going out. Well, isn't that what it's supposed to show? Yes. But it can and should show much more. You'll notice there's no men-

Cash Receipts	
Amounts collected from customers	$372,500
Advances from bank credit line	7,500
Sale of short-term investments	24,000
Total Cash Receipts	404,000
Cash Disbursements	
Paid to creditors	308,200
Payroll and payroll taxes paid	122,600
Purchase of new equipment	45,000
Payments on long-term debt	1,000
Dividend payments	5,000
Total Cash Disbursements	481,800
Net Cash Flow (Drain)	(77,800)
Add balance of cash—beginning of period	42,500
Balance of cash—end of period	($35,300)

Figure 6-1. Statement of cash receipts and disbursements

tion of net income on this report or any attempt to explain the difference between net income and net cash flow—a key question for anyone managing a company. It also doesn't show inflows and outflows grouped by purpose in any meaningful way and there's more information that can be communicated there as well. A variation was once called the Statement of Sources and Applications of Funds, but it was only marginally more useful and is rarely seen these days.

That's why the indirect method was developed, why it's the standard report format used in published annual reports, and why it's the format that comes out of nearly all accounting software programs when you ask for a statement of cash flow. It's a bit harder to understand initially, but the potential for meaningful analysis is far greater. That's why we'll discuss only the indirect method format in this chapter and try to give you a sense of what each line is telling you. If you find you need to read this section over a few times to get the concepts working for you, it will be time well spent.

> **Direct method of presenting cash flows from operat-** Key
> **ing activities** Shows each major class of gross cash receipts Term
> and gross cash payments, summarizing cash outflows and
> inflows. This method may be easier for people without accounting train-
> ing to read. However, it's not considered to have much analysis value.
>
> **Indirect method of presenting cash flows from operating**
> **activities** Begins with net income and adjusts for changes in account
> balances that affect available cash. This method requires some practice
> to learn to read it, but it's much preferred by experts because of the
> wealth of information it contains.

Let's look at the statement of cash flow from The Wonder
Widget Company (Figure 6-2). Notice that the first entry on the
page is Net Income, giving us a clue that this statement will
pick up where the income statement left off. The idea is that net
income is presumed to be equal to net cash flow, except for the
adjustments that make up the details of this statement. Notice
also that the entries on the page are divided into three sections—Operations, Investing, and Financing. These are the three
principal areas of activity for most companies.

Let's explore the activities of Wonder Widget for June 2003
and see what we can learn from its cash flow reporting. We've
slipped in a couple of transactions that our early stage company
might not be able to pull off just yet, like long-term borrowing,
but this gives us more opportunity to explain the kinds of
entries we might see on a more fully developed company's
report. We've also added a few words of commentary to each
line on the report, to help you understand the nature of the
transactions that created the need for the adjustment; we'll
comment on those further in the respective sections that follow.

Cash from Operations—Running the Business

Operations is the process of running the company, with all the
related cash flows, such as buying and selling goods and services, manufacturing, paying employees, etc. In the simplest of sit-
uations, involving only the day-to-day operation of the compa-

Operations		
Net Income		$19,200
Adjustments		
Add back depreciation—no cash paid for this	7,500	
Increase in accounts receivable—more sold than collected	(125,600)	
Decrease in prepaid expenses—amortized, but no cash paid	1,500	
Decrease in inventory—cash raised by lowering stock on hand	10,600	
Increase in accounts payable—cash borrowed from creditors	28,500	(77,500)
Cash flow provided by (used for) Operations		(58,300)
Operations		
Capital expenditures—cash invested in new equipment	(45,000)	
Short-term investments sold—net proceeds from sale	24,000	
Cash flow provided by (used for) Investments		(21,000)
Financing		
Increase in bank debt—new short-term borrowing from bank	7,500	
Net reduction in long-term debt—payments made on long-term loans	(1,000)	
Dividends paid to stockholders—cash paid out to owners	(5,000)	
Cash flow provided by (used for) Financing		1,500
Net Cash Flow (Drain)		(77,800)
Add balance of cash—beginning period		42,500
Balance of cash—end of period		($35,300)

Figure 6-2. Statement of cash flow, April 2003 (indirect method)

ny, this is the conversion of net income into net cash flow. You'll see how that happens as this chapter unfolds.

Net Income

The first line is net income because, as we've noted, a prime objective of this report is to show the differences between net income and net cash flow. This number should be the same as the net income amount shown on the income statement. Next, we list as adjustments all the operating items that had an impact on cash that were not included in the income statement.

Add Back Depreciation

Do you remember the way equipment and other assets are charged to expense? Depreciation—the gradual charging of the cost to expense over their useful life, as discussed in Chapter 5—is recorded each month after the asset is put into use, yet no cash changes hands as a result of those depreciation entries, because the cash was all paid out when the asset was bought. So the monthly charge for depreciation expense must be removed from reported net income, in effect *increasing* income by the $7,500 that had no effect on cash. (We call these *non-cash items.*) So depreciation expense is always added back to net income, usually as the first adjustment on this report.

Increase in Accounts Receivable

Some of the customer balances Wonder Widget had at the beginning of the month were collected during the month and some were not. Similarly, some of the sales made during the month were paid for by their customers, although typically credit sales on 30-day terms would not (retail cash businesses aside, of course). At the end of the month, the company had some of the opening customer balances still outstanding, as well as some of the new balances.

Look at this another way. If all their opening customer balances and all sales during the month were collected in cash, there would be no ending accounts receivable and the month's cash receipts from customers would be equal to their opening balances plus sales. However, since there were still outstanding balances at the end of the month, the amount of cash they took in must be reduced by those outstanding balances. Here it is as a formula:

beginning accounts receivable + sales − ending accounts receivable = cash collections

But remember that sales are all included in net income; this adjustment is to show how much of the period's sales must be removed from the presumption of cash flow because the cash

!CAUTION!

/\ /\ /\

A Negative Adjustment for Accounts Receivable Is a Red Flag

This small gem of information is of huge importance if cash management is important to the company, because the amount of accounts receivable means cash that has to come from somewhere— cash that will stay out of the company's reach until those balances are collected. If this happens every month, the balance sheet could be growing, sales could be growing, but the company could be slowly slipping into insolvency, as Wonder Widget was in Chapter 5.

Now, that may be OK if their sales grew as much or more, because a growing company that sells on credit—and does reasonable cash flow planning—should normally expect its accounts receivable to grow as its sales grow. But if sales were flat or down from the prior month, and the company *still* loaned money to its customers, that would mean its collection effort was not adequate and its customers are using up the company's working capital by delaying payment to them.
Remember: any increase in receivable balances greater than the monthly increase in sales is an interest-free loan to your customers. And that sinks companies.

for them wasn't actually received. Now the formula might look like this:

sales + (beginning accounts receivable – ending accounts receivable) = cash collections

Notice that the calculation in parentheses effectively converts sales to cash collections by comparing the balances of accounts receivable from the beginning of the month and the end of the month. If the company sold more to its customers during the month than it collected, this adjustment would be a negative or bracketed amount, showing less cash inflow than what was presumed by net income. In other words, in our example the company loaned its customers $125,600 out of cash, so cash was reduced as a result.

Decrease in Prepaid Expenses

In our Chapter 3 discussion of prepaid expenses, we talked about the up-front payment for things that have an extended period of value, like insurance. And we noted that such payments are expensed over their period of value by periodic charges to net income, charges that do not require additional payment of cash. So each monthly charge to income for a portion of prepaid expense is a noncash charge, just like depreciation, and the company would add it back to net income in the same fashion.

Of course, in the same month the company might also pay an insurance premium for the coming year and make a big cash disbursement that would not be charged to expense, the opposite of the amortization adjustment above. In this case, it would reduce net income for cash paid out that was not reflected in the income statement; this would be a negative adjustment, showing additional outlay of cash beyond what the income statement contains.

This line in the statement of cash flow is the net of these two kinds of adjustments. The decrease of $1,500 in Figure 6-2 indicates that the noncash expense for amortization was larger than any amounts paid out for new prepaid items. As with accounts receivable, the change in the balance of prepaid expenses on the balance sheet from beginning to end of month is a quick way to calculate the net effect of this adjustment on cash flow.

Decrease in Inventory

You may be able to visualize this one without too much effort. If Wonder Widget purchased only the merchandise it sold during the month—sort of the way Dell Computer tries to do it—it would need to keep essentially no inventory of goods on hand. Since that doesn't work for most companies—and even Dell has *some* inventories—the change in inventory balances works on the cash account just like accounts receivable.

Remember: the income statement includes the cost of all inventory sold during the month. The inventory adjustment on the statement of cash flow is needed *only* if the beginning inventory balance changed by the end of the month, indicating the company purchased inventory it didn't sell during the month

Inventory up, Sales Not: Another Red Flag for Cash!

A company will add inventory when it anticipates growing sales. Toy companies add inventory all year long for their big holiday selling season. But that costs cash—and inventory doesn't return to cash for a long time. It must first become sales and accounts receivable before it becomes cash again. If inventory is going up and sales forecasts aren't growing accordingly, the company may be investing too much in goods that might never become cash. Liquidating old inventory is a very poor way to raise cash—and it almost always results in a loss on the income statement and in cash flow.

or sold inventory it didn't have to purchase that month. As a formula, it would look like this:

beginning inventory + cost of goods purchased and not yet sold – cost of goods sold that were purchased previously = ending inventory

Or, if we rearrange the pieces a bit:

(cost of goods purchased and not yet sold – cost of goods sold that were purchased previously) = (beginning inventory – ending inventory)

So, the cash flow adjustment must deduct the cash cost of any inventory added to beginning inventory balances (meaning that inventory went up during the month, costing cash). Conversely, the cash flow adjustment would be positive if the inventory balance were reduced during the month, indicating the company sold some goods out of beginning inventories and did not have to spend cash to replace them.

Increase in Accounts Payable

The last operating item in this report is accounts payable, amounts owed to creditors of all kinds. Since payment of liabilities requires use of cash, any change in a company's accounts payable means it has either used cash to pay off some trade obligations not included in the income statement or increased the amount owed to creditors, thus borrowing money from creditors for use in the company.

If a company uses cash to pay down its creditor balances,

as Wonder Widget apparently did with $28,500 of its cash, the result is a lower payables balance at the end of the month than at the beginning of the month and net income is adjusted downward; a negative adjustment shows that this payment activity reduced cash. If the company had ended the month with higher accounts payable than at the beginning, it would have effectively borrowed more money from its creditors than it needed to pay the month's expenses; the adjustment would be a positive one for the amount of cash thus raised. Again, the change in accounts payable from beginning to end of the month is a quick way to calculate the amount of this adjustment, whether it increased or decreased cash available to the company.

Cash for Investing—Building the Business

Investing is concerned with plowing back into the business some of the cash generated by the business in order to grow. Growth investment can include buying equipment for expansion, buying or selling investment assets, and other activities that enable the company to increase its ability to do more business.

Capital Expenditures

The most common description you're likely to see in this section is the amount spent for equipment used in the business, typically called *capital expenditures*. Such expenditures for the assets used in the business require cash, but are not charged to income. (Refer to the discussion of depreciation above.) Therefore the cash paid out for them is shown here as a reduction in cash. In our example, Wonder Widget bought $45,000 in equipment for use in its operations and paid cash for it. Since

> **Key Term**
>
> **Capital expenditures** A term used to describe amounts spent for all fixed assets (as discussed in Chapter 3) that are not charged to expense when purchased, but are recorded on the company's balance sheet—that is, they're *capitalized*—and then depreciated over the amount of time they are used by the business. Also may be identified by the shorthand phrase "CapEx."

the asset purchase is not an expense, its cash cost appears as a capital expenditure.

But maybe the company borrowed the money for the equipment. What then? The statement considers that purchasing equipment and borrowing money for the purchase are two separate decisions, so they're treated separately in the statement details. Although the company might have recovered that cash by borrowing the money to purchase this equipment, this was still a commitment of cash and so it appears here as a deduction from the cash produced by net income. Had the company financed the purchase, an offsetting item would appear in the Financing section of this statement. You'll notice there is no large influx of cash in the Financing section, so it appears that Wonder Widget did not borrow money for this purchase. Rather, it raised the money from other sources, including its available cash.

Short-Term Investments Sold

Sometimes a company will invest excess cash so that the money will be working for the company until it's needed in operations. Such investments are typically short-term commitments, such as bank certificates of deposit or marketable securities, which the company sells when it needs the cash. Emerging companies with successful public offerings of their stock (more on this in Chapter 12) often raise a lot of cash before they are ready to use it. Large public companies that sell bonds or additional shares of their stock will also have extra cash on hand, destined for some future corporate purpose. Short-term investments are a way to earn income from these otherwise idle cash balances.

When an investment is purchased, it appears as a cash expenditure that would be shown in this section as a reduction in cash. When an investment is sold, as has apparently occurred in our example, the net proceeds of the sale—*except for the gain or loss on the sale*, which is in the statement of net income—become an additional source of cash. Wonder Widget raised $24,000 in this fashion, presumably to partially pay for its equipment purchase.

Other Examples of Investment Items

There are other kinds of transactions that would appear in this statement if the company engaged in them. Notable examples include the following:

- acquiring or selling off other companies, subsidiaries, or business segments
- purchasing land for future expansion
- buying or selling long-term investment assets

Cash from Financing—Capitalizing the Business

Financing is activity to raise money to pay for operations and investments when operations alone do not generate sufficient cash. When a company is expanding and needs more cash than it can raise internally, outside financing is an option. Selling stock in the company to investors, borrowing money from banks or other lenders, and repaying borrowed money are all activities involved in financing.

Increase in Bank Debt

Wonder Widget has succeeded in borrowing $7,500 from a bank, perhaps all it could get to help with the equipment purchase. We can't tell the purpose of the loan by looking only at this report, but we can see that it resulted in an increase in cash during the month.

Of course, if we look further we can see if the company actually borrowed more than $7,500 and used some of that cash increase to repay other loans, which would reduce cash. This line shows the net result of all such transactions, although the report could just as easily have two lines, one for new money borrowed—an increase in cash—and another line for repayments to the bank—a decrease in cash.

How do we answer this analysis question? A quick look at the Wonder Widget balance sheet from Chapter 3 reveals it does have short-term bank loans on the books, so it likely made payments on those loans, which would appear in this section of the report. If we were to prepare a longer form of this report, we might expand it to show both sides of these transactions on separate lines, thus providing additional information to readers.

Net Reduction in Long-Term Debt

This item is not unlike the bank loans items in the way it flows through the report. Additional borrowings increase cash; repayments reduce cash. The separate classification and different labels simply reflect the fact that long-term debt is shown on a different line on the balance sheet, so it is typically shown on a separate line in the statement of cash flow, to help the reader associate the two statements when reading the company's financial report. In this particular month, the company made a $1,000 payment on its long-term debt and did not borrow any more money in this category, so the net change is a reduction of $1,000. We can't be perfectly certain of this from the short format in our example, but logic tells us that a net change in cash of so small an amount was unlikely to include anything other than a monthly payment. A quick look at the balance sheets for this month and the month before (March 2003 in our example) would confirm our notion that no new debt was incurred.

Dividends Paid to Stockholders

A profitable company will often elect to pay a distribution of profits to its owners. A corporation will make that distribution in the form of a dividend on the shares of stock held by its stockholders, as in our example. Since such distributions are almost always in cash and they are not expenses that would appear on the income statement, this is the only place such payments may appear.

Net Cash Flow (Drain)

This is the sum of all the entries preceding it. It should always be equal to the actual change in cash balances from the beginning to the end of the period of the report. That's why the final step in this statement is to add to this line the beginning bal-

Dividends Come from Profits, Not Losses!

You'd have to ask yourself why a new company without strong cash flow would pay a dividend—and that would be a good question to ask Wonder Widget's board of directors, in view of its cash position. Since the directors are probably also the owners, this could have been a self-serving act that was not in the best interests of the company but in the interests of the owners personally. Such errors in judgment are sometimes made in privately owned companies run by their owners, for whom personal cash flow problems often impact their companies. As we've seen in the past couple years, even the largest companies can fall victim to the bad judgment of their top executives/stockholders. While this decision was not necessarily bad, you should ask yourself the question whenever dividends are not clearly coming from profits that have been earned.

ance of cash—which should have appeared on the prior month's balance sheet—and arrive at a grand total that's the new ending balance of cash—which should appear on the balance sheet of the month being reported on. In this fashion the statement of cash flow is tied into the balance sheet just as it was tied into the income statement from the first line. This little step helps to ensure that every transaction has been accounted for on one or the other of these reports.

Using This Report Effectively

You've seen how each of the major activities of a company can affect cash flow in a significant way. The statement of cash flow is intended to make those effects easily visible, so that readers of a company's financial reports can identify and address negative impacts and preserve positive impacts on cash. This report can be longer or shorter than the example used here, but it should include an adjustment line for every item on the balance sheet that has changed, except for cash itself.

You really cannot understand the cash flow activities of a company without this report or, as an alternative, without substantial detailed analysis of its cash records. Sometimes this report will indicate that still more detailed analysis is needed to answer questions that it raises, but it's better to raise those questions than to be unaware of them. In Chapter 7 we'll look at additional ways this information can be presented to give us an even better understanding of cash flow without the hard work.

Manager's Checklist for Chapter 6

❏ The statement of cash flow fills a critical information need: it analyzes all the reasons that net income didn't produce an equal increase in cash in the bank. It's by far the easiest way to get that information.

❏ Cash is needed to finance customer purchases on credit. If accounts receivable is growing faster than sales, it's a cash drain for the company. This is often the largest cash requirement a growing company will have, and it cannot be ignored without risking impairment of essential working capital.

❏ Inventory is the second largest consumer of cash, and cash invested in inventory takes the longest time to be converted back into cash again. If inventory is growing faster than sales and expected future sales are not increasing correspondingly, the company may be wasting its cash and risking future losses on liquidation of old inventories.

❏ Investments in the company, purchases of assets, borrowing, and other activities to finance company operations and growth are activities that usually involve significant amounts of cash. They are most easily seen and tracked in the statement of cash flow.

Critical Performance Factors and Productivity

Critical Performance Factors:
Finding the "Hidden" Information

Now that you're familiar with all the foundation financial statements that most companies use, you may feel pretty well prepared to understand how well a company is doing financially. And you'd be right, compared with most folks. Since most companies don't prepare all those reports every month and most people who read them don't really understand how much information they contain, you are decidedly ahead of most of your peers in this area. And since you don't likely plan to become a financial analyst, that should cover you pretty well. Why would you even want to go digging for "hidden" information that isn't on the basic financial reports? Why critical performance factors (CPFs)?

The answer is ... "It all depends."

If you run the company, it's because your banker will want to see the information. And your other lenders. And your auditors. And the securities analysts who follow your stock. They will all want to see them, because they want to see what's behind the basic financial statements, the strengths and weaknesses of your company that don't appear in bold type in your statements or the accompanying footnotes. And if they go there, you want to be there first, to see that information before they do.

If you're employed by the company, it's because you may want to know how healthy it is beyond the rumors in the halls and the muffled comments in the washroom. If the company is in dire straits and needs to cut costs tomorrow, you might want to know that, if possible. If the foundation is like the Rock of Gibraltar, but it doesn't yet show up in the income statement, that just might influence how much you put into your 401K or the company pension fund.

If you've invested in the company or are considering investing in it, it's because you can readily see how knowing things that other people don't know, good or bad, can make you a hero or keep you from being the last one out the door. Hidden information is what many insiders make their buy and sell decisions on—and what people in general probably couldn't understand if they had it. But with these tools you can.

OK, so the answer isn't "It all depends." The real answer is that you *always* want to have this information, because it gives you insights, options, and alternatives that you aren't going to get anywhere else. It gives you information that gets to the root causes of problems only hinted at in the basic financial statements, information that can give you not only the sources of problems, but also important clues as to the solutions.

What Are CPFs? Do They Mix with Water?

CPFs are the performance metrics that enable us to look at the relationships in a company's financial numbers in a new way. They are best accompanied by a benchmark, a standard against which the metric is compared to see if the company is doing better or worse than was expected or hoped for. The result is an insight that we didn't have previously about an area that's important to us.

Price/Earnings Ratio

An investor follows a stock's price/earnings (PE) ratio, which is a CPF of the stock's price performance.

If you've ever bought one of those investment newsletters, the ones that charge you to tell you how to invest what you have left after paying their subscription fees, you've heard the term PE ratio many times. It's the relationship between the price of a share of stock and the slice of the earnings of the company attributable to that same share of stock. This is a favorite way of estimating if the price of the stock is too high in relation to the amount of money the company is earning. You might read that Wal-Mart carries a PE ratio of 32 and the analyst considers it overpriced at anything over 20. In this example, the metric is PE ratio, the current reading is 32, and the benchmark is 20. You quickly have a lot of information about the company's earnings that didn't appear on its income statement. That's the power of a CPF.

Measures of Financial Condition and Net Worth

These metrics are related to the company's balance sheet. They calculate the company's financial strength as of a point in time (remember the "freeze frame"?) to give us a sense of how well the company has used its resources to build stockholder value.

Current Ratio

This is perhaps the most commonly known CPF in business today, after the price/earnings ratio. The current ratio is usually presented as two numbers separated by a colon. Using the data from Wonder Widget's balance sheet in Figure 3-1, the arithmetic to arrive at the numbers goes like this:

$$\frac{\text{Current Assets}}{\text{Current Liabilities}} = \frac{1,667,000}{819,000} = 2:1$$

This metric is the relationship between current assets (which are cash or will become cash within the next 12 months) and current liabilities (debts that must be paid within the same 12 months). (You'll recognize these terms, "current assets" and "current liabilities," from in the discussion of balance sheets in Chapter 3.) The purpose is to assess the liquidity of the enterprise, its ability to generate cash as needed to maintain operations.

> **Key Term**
>
> **Current ratio** A comparison of current assets and current liabilities, a commonly used measure of short-run solvency—the immediate ability of a company to pay its current debts as they come due. The current ratio is particularly important to a prospective lender or supplier that is considering extending credit.

Since current liabilities must be paid out of current assets, having a ratio of 1:1 should be OK, right? Wrong. Now don't feel too badly, because that would seem logical on the surface, but let's look at this for a moment.

Current liabilities are bills with a firm due date and the requirement to pay them in full—all of them. Current assets probably consist of some accounts receivable and inventory. Do you recall the discussion about these assets in Chapter 3? They don't always deliver 100 cents on the dollar. Sometimes customers pay late and sometimes they don't pay at all. Sometimes inventory sells for full value and sometimes it becomes worthless or simply disappears. So a company needs *more* than $1 of current assets to cover each dollar of current liabilities. Most banks want to see ratios of 2:1 or better to give them adequate reassurance that the business will have the cash needed when it's time to write checks. This standard will vary by industry, of course, because different industries have different working capital risk characteristics.

Quick Ratio

This is a variation of the current ratio, but with a slight twist. It removes inventory from the calculation on the assumption that inventory returns to cash much more slowly, and with more risk, than other current assets. Do you remember the bad things that can happen to inventory while it's sitting around waiting to be sold? And that doesn't count the added time and cost that must be put into raw materials before they can become finished goods and even begin to be sold. So removing inventory results in a total for current assets that will more quickly become cash. This becomes a more conservative version of the current ratio and it's calculated like this:

$$\frac{\text{Current Assets} - \text{Inventory}}{\text{Current Liabilities}} = \frac{1,667,000 - 591,000}{819,000} = 1.3:1$$

Typically lenders will look at the quick ratio rather than the current ratio if they believe a company's inventory carries higher than normal risk or is a higher percentage of current assets than they consider wise. For the same reason as the lenders, a company should keep an eye on this ratio if it carries large inventories, because it increases the risk of loss. If the current ratio should typically be 2:1 or better, the quick ratio might need only to be 1.3:1 or better. Since it will become cash more readily, less of a safety margin is required for prudent management.

> **Quick ratio** A measurement similar to *current ratio*, except that the current assets calculation excludes inventory. It's thus a conservative version of the current ratio.

Days Sales Outstanding (DSO)

We've emphasized prompt collection of accounts receivable numerous times in this book, not because we enjoy being redundant but because it is so vital to so many aspects of a successful business. So it's not too surprising that one of the key measures of liquidity would deal squarely with that issue. Days sales outstanding (DSO) is the calculation of the number of days of average sales yet uncollected in accounts receivable.

The arithmetic looks like this, again using Wonder Widget's balance sheet on Figure 3-1 and its income statement in Figure 4-1:

$$\frac{\text{Monthly Revenue}}{30} = \frac{\text{Accounts Receivable}}{\text{Average Revenue per Day}} = \frac{940,000}{21,667} = 43 \text{ Days}$$

This metric tells you how closely the company is coming to adhering to the collection terms printed on its invoices. Ideally, a company will sell its products or services with 30-day terms and customers will pay them 30 days later, so the DSO would consistently be 30 days. Most companies offer 30-day credit terms, yet the average DSO for companies across the country

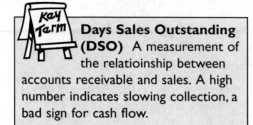

Days Sales Outstanding (DSO) A measurement of the relatioinship between accounts receivable and sales. A high number indicates slowing collection, a bad sign for cash flow.

is said to be in the neighborhood of 45 days, with some companies experiencing even longer delays. With that in mind, a standard anywhere in the 40-to-50-day range is probably acceptable in most cases. Of course, DSO by itself doesn't tell the whole story. To be certain there isn't a problem, this metric should be reviewed along with the age of the accounts.

Inventory Turnover

For all the reasons mentioned before, the faster inventory gets sold, the better for everyone watching the income statement and the bank account. If it's selling, it's usually not getting spoiled, broken, or lost. That's why companies try to keep their inventories as low as possible, consistent with being able to promptly service customer orders. A key metric, therefore, is inventory turnover—how quickly inventory is leaving the plant and being replaced by new inventory. This measurement looks like this:

$$\frac{\text{Annual Cost of Goods Sold}}{\text{Average Inventory}} = \frac{475,000 \times 12}{591,000} = 9.6$$

If Wonder Widget's inventory turnover ratio is 9.6 times, then inventory is being replaced on average 9.6 times a year and there's a little more than one month's inventory on hand at all times (actually 1¼ months' worth, or 12 ÷ 9.6), on average.

You'll note, incidentally, that we didn't give you enough history to compute average inventory or annual cost of sales, so we used what we had, one month's cost of goods sold x 12, and the inventory balance shown on our sole balance sheet. This calcu-

Inventory turnover A measurement of how quickly inventory is leaving the plant and being replaced by new inventory. A high turnover rate means inventory moves quickly, which is good for cash flow and for minimizing inventory losses.

When a DSO of 43 Is Bad

A 43-day DSO isn't so hot if everything is late and getting later!

Here are two examples of companies with accounts receivable, presented based on the length of time the accounts have been outstanding:

	Company A	Company B
Average revenue per day	21,667	21,667
Current, not yet past due	600,000	600,000
0-30 days past due	250,000	40,000
31-60 days past due	70,000	0
61+ days past due	20,000	300,000
Total outstanding	940,000	940,000
DSO	43 days	43 days

Company A show a status of accounts receivable that's typical, as some customers pay on time, others take a while longer, and a few stretch out pretty far. The situation is pretty normal. There's no problem with a DSO of 43 days. Company B typically collects much more promptly than Company A, but nearly a third of its accounts are way out at 61+, clearly indicating they don't intend to pay normally. The DSO is still 43 days, but there's a *big* problem!

Always look at both the DSO and the age distribution of the accounts, the detailed report showing how long customer balances have been outstanding, before concluding that everything is OK. That detailed report is called the *aged trial balance of accounts receivable*.

lation is subject to less misleading fluctuation if you use a broader period of time for this metric.

Measures of Profitability

These metrics attempt to evaluate the company's earnings by calculating various relationships between elements of the income statement and other numbers. The idea here is to measure the company's earnings performance, that is, how well it's keeping its resources working to produce profitable transactions.

Gross Profit Margin

Gross profit is the amount of money earned from selling the product or service and paying the actual costs of making the product or providing the service, as we discussed in Chapter 4. Gross profit margin (or simply gross margin) converts that amount into a percentage of gross revenue. We'll use the income statement from Chapter 4, Figure 4-1, for illustration purposes:

$$\frac{\text{Gross Profit}}{\text{Gross Sales}} = \frac{175,000}{650,000} = 26.9\%$$

Gross margin is an important number because, as noted previously, keeping a company profitable requires that it make a profit on what it sells, before costs of marketing and administration. Watching this metric over time is critical, because there are so many components that typically affect it that cannot be controlled or managed easily. The amount of employee overtime spent to rush a past due order out the door affects gross margin, as does the cost of reworking a manufactured part because an inexperienced worker spoiled it.

> **Key Term** **Gross profit margin**
> Gross profit (net sales minus the cost of goods sold) as a percentage of sales or revenue. Also known as *gross margin*.

Net Profit Margin

Net profit is the amount of money the business has earned after selling its products and paying all the expenses of the business. This is the actual "bottom line." Net profit margin converts that amount into a percentage of gross revenue, which, referring again to the income statement in Figure 4-1, looks like this:

$$\frac{\text{Net Profit}}{\text{Gross Sales}} = \frac{19,200}{650,000} = 3.0\%$$

Net profit margin presents interesting analysis opportunities. By itself, it doesn't tell you much about the profit performance of a business. A net profit margin of 3% in a mature software or drug manufacturing business would be pretty awful, but the same percentage in the supermarket business would be considered phenomenal. The value here,

> **Net profit margin** Net profit as a percentage of gross revenue.

as with so many financial metrics, comes from comparison with a standard. In this case, the meaningful comparisons would be (1) with other companies in the same industry and (2) against a company's own historical profit margins. Both are valuable to different groups, but for different reasons.

If you're part of the management of a publicly owned corporation, you're likely interested mostly in the comparison with other companies. For such companies, net profit margin is published in the financial press and, to some extent, it will affect the price of the company's stock. If you hold stock or options in the company, of course, you may be affected personally as well as professionally.

By contrast, if your company is privately owned and you have a management role in delivering profit performance, you're probably most interested in current performance compared with past performance, because continuous improvement

---

The Growth Curve Significantly Affects Profit Expectations

Note the reference above to a "mature" software or drug business. Now think back to the company life cycle chart in Chapter 2, Figure 2-1. It's important to avoid thinking that start-up or relatively new companies can deliver the same kind of profit performance as successful, mature companies with most of their infrastructure in place, because often they can't. A new company must spend money to establish its initial market presence and its *branding*, to build production capacity, and to strengthen its management team. These costs will often lower its profit margins below those of a more established company that may be inherently less profitable, but that has already absorbed those costs in years past. This is why, to understand the real strength of a company, it's key to access historical trends that may show profit improvement and future business plans that may show the level of profits that are attainable when these costs are over.

in this metric means management is probably doing a pretty good job.

Costs per Sales Dollar

There are various metrics that show costs per sales dollar, such as *sales and marketing costs per sales dollar* and *general and administrative (G&A) costs per sales dollar*. These are just two examples of the kind of metrics that can be applied to any number of operating expense items for which company management wants to tie expense growth to revenue growth. The arithmetic looks like this, if you use our income statement data for one of these calculations:

$$\frac{\text{Sales and Marketing Costs}}{\text{Gross Sales}} = \frac{76,000}{650,000} = 11.7\%$$

This same ratio could be developed for administrative expenses, research and development, or any other grouping of operating expenses. Many companies, once they're established and they have their infrastructure investment behind them, will try to associate growth in certain expense categories with planned revenue growth during the same period. This then becomes a useful way to track progress in those cost control areas.

Measures of Financial Leverage

These metrics are related to the measures of financial condition above in that they are based primarily on the balance sheet. However, they fulfill a specific purpose: determining how well the company is succeeding at using other people's money to improve the amount of resources it has working on producing profitable transactions.

Debt-to-Equity Ratio

Recalling the discussion of ownership in Chapter 3, the assets used in a company are provided either by the owners, through capital investment, or by creditors, through the money they lend to the company. The relationship between those two contributions is an important metric of a company's financial health.

The ratio that tracks that relationship, this time using the balance sheet information in Chapter 3, Figure 3-1, is computed like this:

$$\frac{\text{Total Debt}}{\text{Total Equity}} = \frac{1,267,000}{1,979,000} = 64\% = .64{:}1$$

If a company has too much debt, there is risk that a small reversal of fortunes may wipe out the owners' equity entirely or render the company unable to service its debt. While this by itself may not sink a company, it puts extreme pressure on management to return to profitability or invest more owners' capital in the business. Such pressure has often resulted in involuntary turnover in the management team, particularly at the CEO/CFO level.

By contrast, if the company has too little debt, management risks criticism that it doesn't have enough capital at work earning profits for the company. Do you remember our discussion of leverage in Chapter 3? While too little debt is definitely better than too much debt, it does limit somewhat a company's earning potential, and we've seen how leverage can make a company more profitable, and therefore more valuable.

> **Debt-to-equity ratio** A measurement that compares assets provided by the owners, through capital investment, and assets provided by creditors, through money lent to the company. To calculate this ratio, divide total debt by total equity.

As you can imagine, that there's no "right' number for this ratio. It depends on a number of factors, including these:

- how effectively a company can use additional working capital and put it to work increasing profits by more than the cost of the additional resources
- the amount of debt that is long-term vs. short-term, since long-term debt gives a company more time to put the money to work before having to deliver the added profits to repay the debt

- interest rates that impact the cost of money, since long-term debt is typically borrowed under formal lending agreements that bear interest, as opposed to trade creditors' balances, which are generally interest-free
- how profitable the company can be in its industry, since a low-margin business can ill afford to pay high interest rates for additional capital, while a high-margin, high-growth business may be able to profit handsomely from every dollar it can get.

Interest Coverage

This metric is of use pretty much exclusively to bankers that lend money and to the companies that borrow it. *Interest coverage* attempts to measure how well a company's cash flow will succeed in paying the interest on its interest-bearing debt. The calculation doesn't use actual cash flow. Instead, it uses EBITDA (discussed in Chapter 4) as a stand-in for cash flow and actual interest expense to determine how many times the interest expense is covered by approximate cash earnings for the same period. Here's a computation of interest coverage:

$$\frac{\text{EBITDA}}{\text{Interest Expense}} = \frac{50,000}{5,500} = 9.1 \text{ times}$$

The value of this metric to lenders is pretty obvious. They may even have a minimum acceptable ratio or be closely watching trends here, because this is important to them. They want to know that they have a safe margin to ensure they will not have a nonperforming loan on their hands in the event of a reversal in the fortunes of their borrower, however temporary. The thinking of the lenders is that, worst case, they can at least collect interest until the borrower is again able to make full payments. The borrower probably doesn't look at this number very closely, except because its lenders are looking at it and they might get upset if it gets too low compared with expectations or if the number falls below 8 or 10 times interest expense. If you're the borrower and cash flow is tight, you might want to watch this one closely, to give you a heads-up before your lender calls you. If you're invested in a company with bank debt and a troubling metric here, be prepared for the possibility of an announcement about debt restructuring or some such unless this turns around quickly.

Return on Equity

The last metric in the financial leverage series is one that is most meaningful when evaluating publicly owned companies. *Return on equity* measures

> **Interest coverage** A measurement of a company's ability to pay the interest on its interest-bearing debt through its cash flow (as approximated by its *earnings before interest, taxes, depreciation, and amortization*—EBITDA). To calculate interest coverage, divide EBITDA by interest expense. The lower the interest coverage, the greater the debt burden on the company.
>
> **Return on equity (ROE)** A measurement of the rate of return of the stockholders' investment in a publicly owned company. It's calculated by dividing annualized net income by stockholders' equity.

the rate of return on the stockholders' cumulative investment in the company. Referring this time to both our balance sheet *and*

$$\frac{\text{Net Income (Annualized)}}{\text{Stockholders' Equity}} = \frac{19{,}200 \times 12}{1{,}979{,}000} = 11.6\%$$

our income statement, we come up with this calculation:

Unlike some of the other measures, this one is a bit artificial, for two reasons. First, owners' equity bears no relation to what the owners actually paid for their stake in the company. Second, owners' equity bears no relation to what they could sell it for either. Other than that, no problem!

So is the measurement of return on equity useless? Not at all. It still serves us well as a measure of a company's earning power, even if only a theoretical comparison is possible. The same limitations apply to all companies, so the ratio enables a company-to-company comparison, which is useful when selecting stocks. Also, as with any of these metrics, the pattern of change over time—see "Trend Reporting" below—enables us to see a company's progress against its own history.

Measures of Productivity

These metrics are a little different in that calculating them often requires numbers that don't appear on the financial statements. They're more operationally oriented, intended to measure the performance of particular resources within the organization, e.g. its employees, to see if these resources are delivering the kind of results that will contribute to improved numbers on the income statement and balance sheet.

Backlog of Firm Orders

In my mind, the most important metric that doesn't come out of the company's general ledger is this one. It tells us how much business the company has sold that it has yet to deliver to its customers. There isn't much arithmetic to this one. It comes from the company's order entry system, it's represented in dollars of orders, and it's computed like this:

$$\text{backlog of orders} = \text{all firm orders received} - \text{all orders shipped and invoiced}$$

For companies that ship product orders that take some time to fulfill, such as most manufacturers and many distributors, this is a crucial measure of their immediate future as well as an indicator of the success of their sales team in their efforts to keep the production capacity of the company humming. Like any good metric, it comes with good news and bad news.

If backlog is falling over time, it means the company is not bringing in new orders as fast as it's filling the ones it had. A trend like that cannot continue indefinitely or the company will eventually have no orders to fill. It means either the Production Department is super efficient or the Sales Department is not. Neither is a good thing, even if the company is ringing up nice sales at the time while it ships all those orders leaving the shipping dock.

If backlog is rising over time, that could be either good news or bad news. If Sales is bringing in orders so fast that Production can't fill them, customers will be unhappy and the company

Have You Tried to Get Broadband Service Lately?

When DSL first became available for broadband Internet access, prospective customers waited weeks and often months for their telephone companies to get around to filling their orders— sometimes only to be told they were unable to provide the service because they were out of reach by 50 feet. As competition developed for DSL from cable and satellite service, the wait times got shorter and phone companies built capacity and became more responsive *in order to keep their backlog from disappearing.*

may lose customers. This will tend to hamper the Sales Department's continued success in overwhelming Production, but for all the wrong reasons.

The objective of Sales should be to continue to build the backlog, while the objective of Production—and this includes the salespeople and drivers in the distributors' offices as well as the service providers of service businesses—should be to deliver on orders faster than Sales can bring more in. The role of top management, then, is to beef up either side that is falling behind in this tug of war, so that backlog is where they want it to be. Where should that be? It all depends. I suppose you could say backlog should be measured by how long on average it takes to bring in an order and to fulfill it, in relation to the customer's expectations.

In reality, I can't recall ever hearing a company say its backlog was too high. Too old, maybe. Too difficult to fulfill, sure. Too unprofitable to fret over, unfortunately yes. But too high? Nope, never. Companies use backlog to measure the success of their sales efforts. I recommend to clients they build it into the incentive plans of their top sales and marketing executives and that they track it regularly and visibly.

Order Processing Time

Another metric that doesn't require any complex calculations, but that can have a huge impact on a company's success, is the time to process an order. This one isn't for everyone, but when it fits, it's a great way to build and to measure customer satisfaction. Once a customer has placed an order, he or she has an expectation of when it will be fulfilled. The seller has an obligation to influence that expectation toward alignment with the company's capability and then to meet the expectation. As noted above in the discussion of backlog, if you don't meet your customers' expectations of delivery, you had better be the only source in town—or your customers will soon be shopping for other suppliers.

This measurement is usually presented in terms of days elapsed from the time a company representative receives the order until the order ships to the customer. As you can see, it can be adversely affected by a number of functions within the company—sales, order entry, credit, production, quality control, and shipping, not to mention the delivery service. The goal of management is to coordinate all these activities so people work together toward the mutual objective of satisfying the customer, rather than to try to avoid blame if the order is late.

Sales per Customer, Sales per Employee, Sales per Square Foot of Floor Space

Each of these three metrics measures the productivity of the sales effort, how well a company is spending its sales dollar. They're important measures and easy enough to calculate, although often hard to influence. Each of these is used when appropriate, based on the sales model. All can be useful in a retail environment. Some would not be useful outside of a retail business. Let's look at each of these briefly.

Sales per customer can be useful when a company finds its cost to process an order is fixed or at least controllable. In that case, it can increase profit significantly if it can increase the average amount a customer buys, because there may be little or no increase in the costs of making the sale (beyond the actual cost of the merchandise, of course).

Sales per employee is most useful when the department or company is strongly sales-driven. Retail sales organizations often fall into this category. In some companies, the entire organization is encouraged to think in terms of sales, while in other companies the Sales Department is the prime mover. However this one is used, it helps when assessing the effect on sales of adding another employee or when comparing one branch office with another or one division with another. When applying this measure, CEOs need to be careful to recognize the differences and similarities among departments or divisions. Some business models are different enough that they cannot efficiently be compared on a sales-per-employee basis, and to do so would inhibit one or the other from operating most effectively in its market.

Sales per square foot is a metric used pretty exclusively in retail establishments, where stores must use every foot of space productively, space is limited, and the contribution of a product display can be measured in how much sales it produces per foot of space it occupies. This is very commonly used by the management of chain stores to compare the productivity of one store's management with another. Again, absolutes may not be possible because of the different locations and the demographics of their areas (higher or lower income, younger or older, blue collar vs. white collar, and so on).

Trend Reporting: Using History to Predict the Future

Most people who read financial statements look only at the monthly or annual reports, and most of those reports present their period data in comparison with the immediately prior period or against the same period a year ago. The more enlightening reports compare results against a budget, which is a carefully considered benchmark in its own right. (See Chapter 10 for more on budgets.)

But in all these cases there's a flaw in the lone comparison that can prove dangerous over time: they overlook the fact that a small flaw, a minor deterioration from the prior period, a tolerable budget variance, if repeated over a series of past and future periods, can become a major surprise when taken cumu-latively. When the surprise is a pleasant one, everyone can laugh and say, "How weird we didn't see that earlier!" When the surprise is unpleasant, however, the tendency is to begin a fran-tic search for answers. "How did this happen?" "When did this happen?" "Why didn't we know it was happening?" "Who's responsible?"

What We Learn from Trends

The most important things we learn from studying trends are clues to the future. In high school physics, many of us learned the principles of Newton's first law (the law of inertia): an object in motion tends to continue in motion in the same direction at constant speed unless acted upon by another force. Well, that may not be exactly what your teacher said, but it's close enough for our purposes. Of course, the object your teacher used to make this point didn't have market forces, interest rates, recessions, and human intervention and emotions to bump it around or its path would have been a lot more erratic. So, too, the paths of many of our economic indicators are often erratic, but that doesn't change the validity of studying their trends to begin to estimate where they might go in the future.

As it turns out, a strong sales effort that brings in good sales numbers tends to continue to do so, given no radical changes in its environment. A company whose costs are rising slowly and steadily because it doesn't effectively control them will likely continue to see its costs rise until it takes some action to disrupt the trend. Human nature being what it is, costs are more likely to rise without controls than they are to fall of their own weight, so studying trends of costs is useful to enable management to identify those trends soon enough to keep the cumulative effect within acceptable limits.

The 6-to-12 Rule

We have found that the most effective way to follow trends in a company is to use an easy-to-read format that shows at least

---

**Lessons Learned from the Stock Market—
or Maybe Not Learned**

Much stock market analysis and commentary is based on
the premise that what happened in the past may be projected to some
degree into the future—with all the usual caveats that the analysts
don't guarantee that any of this is true or predictable or even relevant.
We've learned how inaccurate they can be in predicting the future
from the past, but there are ample stacks of evidence to suggest the
premise is true, even if the application is decidedly imperfect. Anyone
who has studied technical stock market analysis can point to countless
examples of stocks acting pretty much like they did before, given similar market influences. The trick is to judge with acceptable accuracy
the variation between past experience and future expectations.

---

six months or six weeks of metrics on a single page as part of a
regularly published, monthly or weekly management report.
How much should you pack onto that one page? If there's too
much information on the page, it will be overwhelming to those
not comfortable with financial reports and it will likely go
unread. If there's too little information on it, it will raise more
questions than it answers, with resulting delays in taking action.

The ideal combination, in our experience, is a page with six
to 12 metrics presented over the past six to 12 periods, along
with the benchmark or standard that is desired for each metric.
That could be the budgeted result at year-end, or the ratio set
out in the covenants of the company's lending agreements, or
the amount needed to take the company to the next level in its
growth. Figure 7-1 shows a representative CPF trend report for
a manufacturing company.

Which Metrics to Track? Where Do You Want to Go This Year?

Which metrics are most meaningful to a company depends on a
series of factors, including management goals and objectives,
problem areas that bear watching, and improvement projects
under way. A sales-driven company may be heavy on the sales-
related indicators, while a company deeply into research and
development of leading-edge products might have metrics relat-

Metric	Actual Results for the Week Ending:											
	8/16/02	8/23/02	8/30/02	9/6/02	9/13/02	9/20/02	9/27/02	10/4/02	10/11/02	10/18/02	10/25/02	11/01/02
Operations												
Orders shipped (Net Sales)	12,430	189,577	59,002	27,748	38,393	131,752	24,645	57,606	71,078	42,012	99,228	11,384
Orders shipped on time	800	19,040	3,402	27,748	741	9,983	17,377	57,326	44,985	13,362	6,594	1,024
Past due orders in house	1,345,920	1,181,612	1,128,172	1,135,331	1,120,594	1,084,906	1,088,123	1,104,272	1,081,075	1,056,700	956,455	949,763
Sales and Marketing												
New quotes issued	1,709,010	524,583	921,760	2,130,817	3,802,839	864,870	3,283,517	2,201,621	3,464,634	2,823,921	712,581	945,168
Beginning backlog	1,900,000	1,926,479	1,783,311	1,743,528	1,724,176	1,828,440	1,718,797	1,737,229	1,689,532	1,641,768	2,367,713	2,333,101
+ New orders booked	38,909	46,409	19,219	8,396	142,657	22,109	43,077	9,909	23,314	767,957	64,616	—
– Shipments to customers (Net Sales)	(12,430)	(189,577)	(59,002)	(27,748)	(38,393)	(131,752)	(24,645)	(57,606)	(71,078)	(42,012)	(99,228)	(11,384)
Ending backlog	1,926,479	1,783,311	1,743,528	1,724,176	1,828,440	1,718,797	1,737,229	1,689,532	1,641,768	2,367,713	2,333,101	2,321,717
Finances and Administration												
Percent of A/R beyond 90 days past due	20%	20%	14%	16%	14%	23%	18%	17%	17%	8%	10%	16%
Percent of A/P beyond 45 days past due	12%	15%	19%	19%	18%	21%	19%	22%	21%	18%	15%	14%
Notes Payable—Bank Loan Balance	500,000	499,445	534,445	484,445	560,000	640,000	705,000	705,000	305,000	375,000	425,000	425,000
Beginning cash balance	35,000	50,324	67,120	130,629	53,791	79,443	1,944	58,118	204,225	60,727	45,941	49,216
+ Receipts	79,827	23,704	90,664	22,542	60,060	32,199	17,066	207,790	374,557	3,720	11,892	13,382
± Bank Credit Line advances	35,000	(555)	35,000	(50,000)	75,555	80,000	65,000	—	(400,000)	70,000	50,000	—
– Disbursements	(99,503)	(6,353)	(62,155)	(49,380)	(109,964)	(189,698)	(25,892)	(61,683)	(118,055)	(88,506)	(58,617)	(55,459)
Ending cash balance	50,324	67,120	130,629	53,791	79,443	1,944	58,118	204,225	60,727	45,941	49,216	7,139

Figure 7-1. Financial trend report

ed to development timetables and costs. Since CPFs are short-term metrics, they primarily relate to improvements desired and controls needed in the current year. Longer-term goals are best set forth in a company's business plan (see Chapter 9) and built into CPFs only for the current year of the long-range plan. However, the name really says it all. They should be *critical* to the business and they should relate to *performance*. Here are some areas to consider for such a report:

- Sales trends—number of orders received, dollar volume of orders received, backlog changes, RFPs responded to, sales per whatever (customer, employee, square foot of floor space, and so forth), sales staff in the field, volume of orders shipped, etc.
- Operations trends—average days to ship an order, over-time or premium hours paid (manufacturers), percent of jobs proceeding on time (job shops), number of orders shipped on time or late, etc.
- Financial trends—DSO for receivables, average payout for payables, cash balances, bank credit line status, invoicing timeliness, financial reporting timeliness, discounts taken vs. available, etc.

While trend reports are most compact if presented in a tabular format, they are often more easily readable by non-financial managers if presented in a graphic format—charts, curves, and lines convey powerful visual images of trends in ways that tables of numbers typically can't. In order to keep such reports to a single page, which is recommended, management may need to choose between a longer list of CPFs to track in tabular format and a shorter list in graphic format.

Manager's Checklist for Chapter 7

❑ Critical performance factors (CPFs) are tools for tracking key indicators of success in a business. They're best accompanied by a benchmark or standard against which they are measured. They must be computed separately, because in most cases they don't appear on the basic financial statements.

❑ CPFs are most effectively used when a company identifies its most sensitive areas in sales, operations, and finance and establishes goals or standards for each area to be improved. Common financial CPFs include measures of financial strength, profitability, liquidity, and leverage. Key operational CPFs include relevant productivity indicators. Key sales CPFs should include sales backlog and sales force performance.

❑ Trends tell us what a single piece of data can never tell us—what the future might look like. The trick is to capture the right CPFs and to present them in six to 12 periodic readings, so that it becomes easier to see where they are going and whether action should be taken to encourage or counter that trend.

Cost Accounting:
A Really Short Course in Manufacturing Productivity

"Cost accounting" sounds a little redundant, doesn't it? After all, isn't all "accounting" about "cost"? Well, yes and no. To folks in the business of accounting and those most familiar with accounting practices, cost accounting is that special branch of the field that deals exclusively with the cost of making or buying a product or service that the company then sells to its customers. Costs that are in the purview of the cost accounting specialists (known affectionately as "cost accountants") are all those costs on the income statement between the revenue line and the gross profit line, referred to in Chapter 4 as cost of sales.

While this area is considerably more complex in a company that conducts manufacturing operations, every company—manufacturing, distribution, retail, or service—needs to understand and manage its gross profit. Remember: gross profit pays for all the other costs of running the company, as well as providing a net profit to the owners. If gross profit isn't managed well, it's very difficult for other segments of the company to make up the

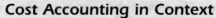

Cost Accounting in Context

Don't let the seeming complexity of this topic deter you—it's really common sense in principle. The concepts are not really complicated; it's just the application that can get a bit confusing if you're applying them to a many-faceted manufacturing operation. I suggest that you apply the examples here to your own company, your own employer, or your own department. I think you'll find the examples make a lot more sense when you have a firsthand experience of the nature of the business that's incurring these kinds of costs.

difference. *Underlying the whole idea of cost accounting is the need of every business to protect and grow its gross profit, while maintaining the quality of its product or service at acceptable levels.*

So this chapter will be devoted to explaining some of the unique attributes of cost of sales and the efforts that go into understanding and controlling them. You will notice as you read this chapter that we're talking primarily about manufacturing companies, because those are businesses for which cost accounting is most challenging, yet most valuable. If you're working in or running a distribution company, a retailer, or a service business, some of the tools and terms we discuss here may seem less important to you. Keep in mind that the principles are universal for every business enterprise.

The Purpose of Cost Accounting—Strictly for Insiders

Amazing as it may seem, many companies don't really know whether or not they're making a gross profit on many of the products they sell. It's a simple matter for a company with even the most fundamental bookkeeping to determine if it's making a gross profit over all of its product sales. But if a company makes a number of products, each with different cost structures and levels of complexity, the managers often don't really know how much each product contributes to—or subtracts from—the overall gross profit.

Cost accounting is the classic example of what outside

observers of a company don't want or need to see. It's a detailed, often complicated process of counting small amounts of money, materials, and labor. Yet these small elements of

Cost accounting An area of management accounting that deals with the costs of a business in terms of enabling the managers to identify, measure, and control gross profit.

cost, when multiplied by the number of units a company makes and sells over a month or a year, become the foundation for the profit that outsiders *are* anxious to see from companies they follow. Cost accounting, then, is the ultimate example of internal management reporting: it's in a form designed for managers to use in running the company and not particularly user-friendly to those unfamiliar with the company or the business.

Are You Making a Profit or Just Building Sales Volume?

I'm sure you remember that old cliché, *"We're losing money on every piece, but we're making it up on volume!"* That clever bit of shtick that makes everyone laugh is not so funny in many of today's companies, particularly the ones that don't have a strong cost accounting analysis function in their financial department. Accounting for all the variety and complexity of costs that go into manufacturing a product today is among the most difficult areas of finance to manage. Part of the reason is that information about cost of sales requires additional levels of data collection, some of it from segments of the company most removed from the financial recordkeeping function, the factory worker. It's on the shop floor that costs are incurred, fabrication decisions are made, and hours are spent productively or wastefully—and it's the factory worker who will ultimately determine if the company has a comfortable gross profit or none at all.

Profit Management Begins with a Timecard and a Bill of Materials

Key to gross profit management, then, is collecting the right information at the right level of detail. One of the most chal-

How to Make More Money by Making Less Product!

Wonder Widget makes two home products, each with identical unit sales. The WW-1000 sells for $425; the custom-made WW-Super 1000 sells for $575. The combined sales of $1 million produces a gross profit of $250,000 each month, or 25%. But the company doesn't know how much each unit costs. They just know that the WW-Super 1000 sells better and, even though it's more difficult to make, they're charging more for it, so they believe the resulting gross profit show that their strategy is sound.

Their financial consultant divides all their cost of sales into two buckets, including the added labor it takes to make the luxury model.

	WW-1000	WW-Super 1000	Total
Selling price per unit	425	575	
No. units sold	1,000	1,000	
Total sales	425,000	575,000	1,000,000
Cost per unit			
Materials	25	25	
Labor	40	240	
Overhead (150% of Labor)	60	360	
Total cost per unit	125	625	
Total cost of sales	125,000	625,000	750,000
Gross Profit	300,000	(50,000)	250,000

Figure 8-1. Gross profit contribution from multiple products

The embarrassed owners of Wonder Widget learned that their best revenue producer was actually losing money, due to the high cost of labor. The real surprise: they could make $50,000 a month more—increase their current gross profit by 20%—if they simply stopped making the deluxe model!

lenging aspects of this is capturing the time that workers spend on each job or part that they work on—*job costing* or *process costing.* The challenge comes in several forms:

- Convincing workers to accurately measure time on a job or to check out the raw materials they will use—tasks that are not often to their liking and not always in the skill sets for which they were hired.
- Convincing workers that the purpose of the detailed time-keeping is to cost out the products, not to keep track of how much downtime they have on the job.
- Convincing supervisors that the time their workers spend reporting time and materials data instead of working on another job is productive.
- Teaching accounting departments how to collect the information accurately, use it properly to calculate the labor cost component of the company's products, and then produce meaningful reports for management.

These are the fundamental data collection tools of job cost accounting:

- A *bill of materials* that enables the company to identify the materials required to manufacture a particular job.
- *Timecards* or *timesheets* for manufacturing employees who work directly on products, broken down by product

---

Job costing Collecting costs for a manufacturing process that's geared to producing products in small lots, or jobs, and assigning costs to those jobs. Jobs may be customized to the customer's requirements, as in a machine shop, or small lots of products for selling later from stock.

Process costing Collecting all costs incurred in a continuous process or processing department, and then averaging these costs over all units produced in that department. This is a mass production kind of operation, such as might be used in making chemicals, gasoline, or textiles. It's different because the nature of the product is different. Instead of specifically identified lots of production, there's a continuous flow, with the final output being complete only when the process is stopped, rather than when the order for X units is filled.

or stages of a product.

- A *materials requisition form* on which is recorded all the materials actually issued to the job, including materials that might have been put into production and then damaged or scrapped and the materials then issued to replace them. These details may be later transferred to a job cost sheet.
- The *job cost sheet*, either paper or electronic, that follows a job through the factory and on which actual production costs are recorded as they are incurred. This may include labor details, precluding the strict need for timecards except as an audit check that all hours paid for were charged to jobs or otherwise accounted for appropriately.

While individual companies may have their own versions of these tools, the objective remains the same: to accumulate, on the one hand, the labor and materials that were intended to be consumed to complete the job and, on the other hand, the labor and materials that were actually consumed to complete the job. The differences will later be analyzed to help managers understand why the actual costs incurred differed from the expected costs. See "Manufacturing Cost Variances" later in this chapter for more insight into this kind of analysis.

Bill of materials A listing of all the individual parts and components that go into the manufacture of a product, including how many of each item of raw materials. This document is used to purchase and then assemble the pieces to produce a given quantity of finished goods.

Process costing, by contrast, is much simpler, due to the *continuous* nature of the manufacturing process. The accounting department collects all the costs incurred by a particular manufacturing department for each manufacturing process carried out in that department and groups them into essentially two categories: direct materials and conversion cost.

Conversion cost is the sum of all the direct labor and manufacturing overhead costs that belong to that department and that process. Dividing the total costs charged to that manufacturing department by the total number of units the department's efforts produced gives us the unit cost of all units produced during the period being

Direct materials Those raw materials that go directly into making the product. The direct materials to manufacture a chair, for example, would include wood, fabric, screws, and glue. (For ease of accounting, some minor costs may not be assigned directly but rather may be grouped into manufacturing overhead.)

measured. The final unit cost is equivalent to the unit cost arrived at in a job costing environment. The difference is that a continuous process does not permit the individual collection of costs by unit during the process, a factor that somewhat limits the analysis potential later on.

Conversion cost The sum of all the direct labor and manufacturing overhead costs that belong to that department and that process.

Direct labor The cost of wages paid to workers who are directly employed in manufacturing products or in providing the services for customers. On the shop floor, it's the labor of the machinist or the welder. In a consulting firm, it's the time of the consultant who's working with the client. In a distribution firm, there may be little or no direct labor, as products are generally purchased in finished form.

Manufacturing overhead All the costs necessary to operate the business that are not classified as direct labor or direct materials. Often referred to as *indirect costs*, these may include rent and insurance, utilities, the janitorial service, and the supervisors who oversee the direct labor workers but who do not work on jobs directly themselves. All these indirect costs are necessary for the manufacturing process, but they are not charged directly to specific jobs. Instead, they're grouped together and then allocated to all the jobs or products in some manageable way. Allocation is most often based on a factor directly related to the work produced, such as direct labor hours worked on the job or direct labor dollars charged to the job.

Fixed and Variable Expenses in the Factory

In any department of every company, including the manufacturer's shop floor, there are costs that do not change from day to day and there are costs that are changing constantly, depending on the company's level of activity. Understanding costs that change and those that don't is important to the manager's ability to manage the costs for which he or she is responsible.

Costs that essentially remain unchanged even though the business increases its volume of sales are called *fixed* costs. Such costs may be more easily predicted and managed, because they stay pretty much the same. An example is the rent on a building that is occupied under a long-term lease. For the most part, that monthly lease payment will remain unchanged for the life of the lease, predefined increases aside. Another example is depreciation expense on an asset, which will remain constant until the asset is removed from service, assuming it lasts as long as intended.

Costs that increase in direct relationship to sales volume are called *variable* costs. For example, a 10% increase in sales will result in a 10% increase in variable costs. You can see that direct materials and direct labor would be variable—the more units you make, the more of those costs you would incur. Packaging materials used in shipping the finished goods would also vary with production levels.

Costs that increase in relation to sales but at a slower pace, for example 5% for each 10% increase in sales, are said to be *semi-fixed* costs, meaning they have aspects of variable costs and also aspects of fixed costs. For example, a manufacturing scrap pickup service might accept larger amounts of scrap without raising its prices for pickup until it needs to send a larger truck and two operators. Then it might increase the price and keep it fixed for a while, until the larger truck can no longer haul more scrap away. The cost over time becomes semi-fixed as sales, and therefore manufacturing scrap, increase.

We try to label every cost element as either fixed or variable because we're trying to understand how costs behave in certain circumstances, for example:

> **Fixed costs** Those costs that essentially remain unchanged even though the business increases its volume of sales.
>
> **Variable costs** Those costs that increase in direct relationship to sales volume.
>
> **Semi-fixed costs** Those costs that increase in relation to sales but at a slower pace. Semi-fixed costs have aspects of variable costs and also aspects of fixed costs.

- If variable costs are increasing faster than sales, there is inefficiency in the process that management needs to identify and correct, because variable costs should never grow faster than sales under normal conditions.
- If costs identified as fixed are rising unexpectedly as sales grow, it is good to know that this should not be caused by increasing sales volume, and the cause should therefore be investigated.
- If costs identified as variable are not rising proportionately with sales, the cause should be investigated, because there may be unrecorded expenses that will distort reporting in the month being reviewed (costs too low) and in the month when they finally get recorded (costs too high).
- Knowing these characteristics enables us to budget more accurately, particularly if we are planning for the possibility of different levels of sales and must be prepared for several possibilities. See Chapter 10 for a discussion of flexible budgets.

However, it's well to keep in mind this simple rule: *All costs are fixed in the short term and all costs are variable in the long term.*

In other words, regardless of the label you put on it, any cost can be reduced by effective management, given sufficient time. In the case of a company's building lease payments, "sufficient time" may mean at the expiration of the lease. Most costs can be modified in a much shorter timeframe, even those we call fixed.

By contrast, even the most variable of costs, such as the labor that goes directly into making a product that will be sold immediately (like the amazing Wonder Widget in Chapter 5), cannot be changed instantly. Labor reductions typically require giving reasonable notice, providing termination pay, overcoming resistance to losing skilled workers, and perhaps other factors that effectively stretch out the time it will take to reduce the net cost to the company.

So, the terms "fixed" and "variable" are not entirely accurate. However, financial managers and the users of their information, as well as production planners and managers, adopted the terms in order to create a framework for approximating how these costs will act. Why? To enable them to predict future cost relationships and thereby manage the bottom-line outcomes of their actions at various sales volumes.

> ### Don't Get Stuck on Labels
>
> An effective manager thinks outside of the categories of "fixed" costs and "variable" costs. Don't assume that you can't reduce fixed costs or that variable costs will be easy to reduce. For example, sometimes it's possible to reduce costs by converting fixed costs to variable costs through outsourcing services or renting equipment as needed. Or you may think that you can reduce the time it takes to assemble a unit, only to find that you're spending more time inspecting and correcting.

Controllable and Uncontrollable Expenses

Now let's look at costs from another angle: our ability to control their movement.

Costs that responsible managers can readily control are called, logically enough, *controllable* costs. Some examples are travel expenses, nonproduction labor costs, most marketing expenses, the amount of inventory purchased, and long-distance telephone charges. Notice that I didn't say that these costs are controllable without consequences, only that they're controllable, which means a manager can make and implement a conscious decision to reduce the expenditure in these areas. Even though the company may lose the benefits to be gained from incurring these costs, they're still controllable because managers *can* lower or eliminate them.

Uncontrollable costs, by contrast, cannot in general be controlled. Examples that readily come to mind include income taxes, depreciation, and rental or lease payments.

Now, you might just notice a parallel with variable and fixed costs. If it didn't come to you immediately, let me point it out here: *All costs are uncontrollable in the short term; all costs are controllable in the long term.*

This is a conceptual truth that will be by and large useless in the accounting department or in the preparation of the budget. But in concept it's important to realize that you're not captive to any costs charged to your department or unit, as long as you are prepared to manage these costs actively and as long as you can accept or ameliorate the consequences of removing those costs, which may include loss of their attendant benefits.

In the production department of a company, controllable costs are those for which managers are held accountable. Cost estimates should be built around the realization that some costs are going to be what they're going to be, regardless of management efforts. If your department has a large drill press on its floor, you'll likely be charged for the depreciation of that machine as long as you're using it. You can't control that cost if you need the drill press to do your job. But by proper preventive maintenance, you can control the repair costs and downtime of that machine—and that's your responsibility if you are running the department.

Stepping outside the manufacturing department for a moment, the concept of controllable and uncontrollable costs applies equally throughout a company's organization structure. Lease payments on property are uncontrollable as long as the lease runs. Once the lease runs out, those costs are again controllable, until you sign another lease, after which they again become uncontrollable. Labor costs are always controllable to a degree, but not totally. You cannot run an organization without people, but you probably can run one with fewer people than are normally employed there, if you're willing to redistribute the essential work and forgo the less essential work that people do.

Consider the possibilities. What if you were able to distinguish between the essential work and the less essential work every day? What if you could focus on minimizing the unessential and expediting the essential? Would your department be more successful? The power of financial analysis is its ability to help identify the financial ramifications of doing just that and to quantify the benefits to be gained in dollars and cents. It is a wonderful tool for helping to make decisions from a place of knowing, rather than estimating or, worse, guessing.

That's why this book was written.

Standard Costs—Little Things Mean a Lot

One of the challenges of financial reporting for cost accounting purposes is determining the actual cost of a unit of finished goods that was produced during the month, in time to issue a financial statement within a reasonable timeframe after the end of that month. Accounting departments are sometimes criticized for issuing financial reports too far after the accounting month is over, when the reports are of little value in attempting to manage the succeeding month (or two, in some cases). Financial statements that take several weeks or more to prepare may not be available soon enough to help managers adjust their performance in the next month. Lessons learned from January reports issued at the end of February cannot be put into use until perhaps March, leaving January's mistakes to be repeated in February. In a fast-moving or highly competitive or slim-margin business, that may not be acceptable to alert management teams. Thus, in recent years technology advances have fostered the growth of "real-time" accounting—systems that collect accounting information continuously and provide selected management reports on demand, without the need to formally "close the books."

In the manufacturing environment, the short-term answer to this need has traditionally been *standard costing*, a term that means using standard costs in lieu of actual costs in the accounting for individual manufacturing steps. Standard costing is a way to estimate the actual cost of a unit for purposes of prompt financial reporting, while still leaving a way to return for more detailed analysis later. Standard costing is a way to carry the budgeting process down to the components of unit cost, so that a company can budget for units of direct labor and raw materials for each unit of finished goods that it plans to produce.

We'll cover budgeting and variance analysis in some detail in Chapter 10, and we'll return to the subject of standard costing, a common method of budgeting the unit costs of production. There's a strong connection between budgeting and standard costing; the commonality will be very evident in the discussion of variance analysis.

> **Standard costing** A management tool used to estimate the overall cost of production, assuming normal operations. Standard costs, rather than actual costs, are used in accounting for steps in a process, assuming an efficient plant operating at normal capacity. The standard costs and actual costs are then compared and causes of variances are explained in terms of price or quantity.
>
> *Key Term*

Manufacturing Cost Variances—Analysis for Action

Using standard costing enables a manufacturer to budget the unit costs of production and to compare actual costs with standard costs in its financial reporting. The benefit of such reporting is not simply seeing whether the two agree or not or even by how much they disagree. The power of standard costing is in analyzing those differences and using that information to enable managers to change what they're doing, in order to make the business optimally profitable. That analysis is called *variance analysis*, meaning the analysis of variances, or differences, to enable managers to learn how to eliminate them.

> **Key Term**
>
> **Variance analysis**
> Process of identifying, measuring, and investigating causes of significant differences (variances) between budget expectations and actual results. Variances can be calculated according to time, volume, cost, efficiency, and price.

The advantages of standard costing include the following:

- helping to more easily estimate inventory value and product cost
- enabling price setting and contract bidding based on realistic costs
- permitting performance measurement and evaluation based on standards
- quickly identifying problem areas through the principles of management by exception
- identifying causes of unsatisfactory performance so that corrections can be made

We'll discuss variance analysis in some detail in Chapter 10, because variance analysis is the principal tool for getting the most value out of budgets in general, but it has particular application in manufacturing, when standard costs are used, and so it belongs in this chapter as well.

In standard costing, there are two basic kinds of variances, or differences from established standards: *price* variances and *usage* variances. Price variances occur when materials or labor used in production cost the company more per unit than was projected when the standards were set. Usage variances occur when the production run

> **Management by exception** A system of management in which standards are set for operating activities. The actual results are then compared with those standards, and any differences that are considered significant are brought to the attention of the managers, along with the reasons for the differences and recommended corrective action, if appropriate.

consumes more of the materials or labor than was planned.

For example, consider the example excerpted from Wonder Widget's weekly manufacturing variance report (Figure 8-2).

Component	No. units produced	Standard per unit	Actual per unit	Variance
Super Widget model 4000 power switch	1,000			
Labor hours per unit produced		1.2 hours	1.5 hours	.3 hours
Labor cost per hour		$25.00	$28.00	$3.00
Labor cost per unit produced		$30.00	$42.00	$12.00

Figure 8-2. Report of manufacturing cost variances

In this example, actual labor cost per unit was $42.00 (1.5 hours at $28.00 per hour). The standard per unit for this switch was $30.00 (1.2 hours at $25.00 per hour). The total unfavorable variance for 1,000 units was $12,000 ($42.00-$30.00 times 1,000 units). That information by itself is interesting, but not particularly useful. It might be difficult to give a plant supervisor that information and expect an informed plan to eliminate the variance. But let's look at what happens when we analyze the components of the variance (Figure 8-3).

Now we know the cause and we know what each kind of variance is costing us. We can approach the supervisor about getting the time back to the standard of 1.2 hours per unit labor

Nature of the Variance	Unit variance	Factor	Amount per unit	Amount of variance
1,000 Units Produced				
Time—more time was used than the standard	.3 per unit	$25.00	$7.50	$7,500.00
Price—labor rate was higher than the standard	$3 per hour	1.5 hours	$4.50	$4,500.00
Total variance accounted for				$12,000.00

Figure 8-3. Analysis of cost variances

or finding out if the standard should be increased because it just takes more time to make these things right. And we can approach the human resources manager to find out why we paid more than standard wages for our labor, e.g., we hired overqualified people, the market has gotten tight for those we need, or we didn't do a thorough enough search for workers within our price range.

This same thought process can be carried out in the analysis of materials variances as well.

Now we have a plan of action and we know the managers with whom we should talk about carrying out the plan. That's what standards can do for a manufacturing company, *if* the managers know what a unit costs and *if* they know what it should cost. This now becomes a powerful management tool for controlling the unit cost of the switch, which contributes directly to the gross profit line on Wonder Widget's income statement.

And that's a good thing.

Manager's Checklist for Chapter 8

❏ Cost accounting is about protecting and growing gross profit by understanding and managing the details of the cost of sales, the costs incurred in producing revenue.

❏ Knowing the costs and gross profit margins on each product a company sells is a critical tool for managing overall gross profit. This is true for all kinds of businesses, but it is more challenging for a manufacturing company because of the complexity of the business.

❏ Cost accounting is possible only when the detailed costs of production are collected at the source, on the shop floor.

❏ Understanding how costs behave is key to controlling them. Tools such as standards and budgets and classifications like "controllable," "variable," and "direct" help us to do that.

❏ Variance analysis is the way managers use standards and management by exception to attempt to reduce variation from predicted outcomes.

Business Planning
and Financing the Plans

Business Planning:
Creating the Future You Want, Step by Step

I n our consulting business we speak to a lot of managers, from for-profit businesses to non-profit organizations. They are busier today than ever before, it seems, and we find more frequent use of planning on both sides. Yet in spite of the apparent trend toward greater use of business planning methods, a common refrain is often heard from harried business managers: "We're too busy running our company to do formal business planning." Even startup CEOs who are creating a whole new company are prone to add, "If potential investors want to look at something, we'll do a plan for them, but we certainly don't need one ourselves. We're clear about where we're going and we don't have the interest or the spare time to write it on paper."

Thus begins still another chapter in the myths of business planning. Table 9-1 includes some of my personal favorites.

Why Take Time to Plan?

Every organization with a goal in mind will develop a plan to get there. Every manager with a job to do will develop a plan to get

The Myth	The Reality
1. Planning is a lot of work; busy managers don't have time for still another task.	Planning actually saves work and time, by helping managers to avoid doing more work than is necessary to reach their goals.
2. Plans are obsolete as soon as they're done.	Plans are dynamic and ever evolving as the business evolves. The best ones get reviewed and modified regularly.
3. Plans must always be long and detailed to be of any value.	Plans need not be any more detailed than the company needs to guide its activities. Some very focused plans for small business will fit on a single page.
4. Business moves too fast to be held back by a plan.	The speed of business is a big reason why plans are important, because we can go very far off the mark in a short time. Plans don't hold managers back; rather, they guide managers' forward movement.
5. Planning is not as important or valuable as doing something productive.	Planning makes what we do more productive by enabling us to avoid doing things that don't contribute to our productivity as measured by end results.
6. We should leave the planning to the planners and let the managers do their work.	Plans done without the substantial involvement of the managers who are making the decisions are largely useless, because they don't reflect reality.

Figure 9-1. Myths of business planning

his or her daily work done. Yet, for the most part, these plans are informal, often people only carry them around in their minds and draw them out as needed, improvising and modifying along the way.

Most people don't think of themselves as planners—and yet they plan every day, either formally or informally. We plan pretty much for the best reasons—because planning helps us to reach goals, whether the goals relate to getting our daily work done, laying out the annual family vacation, or financing our retirement lifestyle.

People who regularly plan in their personal lives sometimes resist planning when their company announces the annual budget or the quarterly business plan review. And yet they are serving the same purpose, to reach desired goals. The company version is different, of course. For one thing, it's usually more formal and more detailed, for several reasons, all related to execution of the plan:

- Execution will require the coordinated efforts of many people.
- Execution will consume substantial, expensive resources.
- The plan will cover multiple, often interlocking and related goals and tasks.

For very much the same reasons, it should be a *written* plan. Putting a plan in writing enables us to gain several important benefits for our planning efforts:

Clarity. It becomes much clearer what must be done and what are the steps to get there. We're less likely to forget something or to have to hastily redirect our efforts to include a missing task, if we've written them down ahead of time. When we carry plans in our heads, funny things sometimes happen. We can change the plan in mid-thought, in case it looks more difficult to reach than we originally thought, and no one will know. We can rationalize with ourselves that 75% is as good as 100%, and no one will hold us accountable for our questionable adjustment of the metric. When it's written, it's crystal clear what the goal was—75% or 100% or whatever—because it's there, on the page in black and white.

Roadmap. If you can remember the last time you tried to find a new street address without a map, you may recall making a few wrong turns, stopping to ask directions, retracing your steps, and generally proceeding more slowly because you weren't sure where you were going. A plan tells you which turns to take and which ones to avoid, and you know ahead of time because you've thought the route through before the journey began.

Fewer wrong turns means less time spent, less money spent, and more results with the same resources.

Communication. We have a means to communicate consistently and easily the goals we want to achieve to anyone who we believe can contribute to our meeting those goals, such as staff, bosses, customers, and suppliers. Goals that are communicated clearly, without ambiguity and confusion, and without the added emphasis of today's emergencies, are more likely to receive support from all those who can help us get there.

Empowerment. In any challenging endeavor, we face goals that seem difficult if not impossible to reach. They may not be impossible, but the idea of getting that far beyond where we are today can seem that way—and when something seems impossible, that can be a self-fulfilling prophecy. By writing our plans down, along with all the critical steps to get there, we effectively break the goals down into small steps. We can then look at each step and clearly see the possibility, even probability, of achieving it. Thus we give ourselves permission to believe the goal is achievable. That permission does powerful things in our minds, shifting what is often the most significant obstacle to success, our own beliefs about the possibilities.

Strategic Planning vs. Operational Planning

There are business plans—and then there are business plans. Let's begin by distinguishing between the two principal types of business plans: strategic plans and operational (or operating) plans. The two will actually look quite different and be written in a different style, because they are intended to be read by different people for different reasons. Every marketing manager knows that a brochure, to be effective, must be customized to its audience. The same holds true for a business plan, whichever type it is. It should always be written to its intended purpose and directed to its intended reader.

A strategic plan is usually more than just a statement of goals. It's a statement of corporate purpose, a request for sup-

> **Business plan** The generic name for a plan written for a business. It will generally include a statement of the overall objective of the plan, the period it covers, and the goals to be achieved. How those ideas are expressed depends on the type of plan.
>
> **Strategic plan** A type of business plan designed to define the overall vision and mission of a business, its strategy and long-term objectives, and some of the key details that might be important to the strategic reader. It will typically be intended to drive the company's strategy for several years and will serve as the basis for the company's operating plan.
>
> **Operating plan** A detailed description of what the company will do to pursue the objectives of its strategic plan for the next operating period, usually one year. It will contain enough detail that the operating managers of the company can use it to guide their daily and monthly activities.
>
> **Financing plan** A special version of a strategic plan written for the express purpose of attracting outside financial resources to the company, usually intended for equity investors, but sometimes written for lenders as well. This version will emphasize the amount of money needed, how it will be used, and how the investors will receive a return on their money.

port, and a call to action. In other words, its purpose usually includes an emotional appeal of some kind. Therefore, the form as well as the content should be aimed at capturing that support.

The purpose of a strategic plan is to guide the overall direction of an organization, to define its grand purpose, what it ultimately wants to achieve, and the general strategies it will use to get there. This might include the definition of its market and its product categories and the ways in which it will change the lives of the buyers in its intended market. It will also define the long-range goals of the organization and provide a segue to the shorter-term and more detailed activities that will be laid out in the operational plans.

The strategic plan typically doesn't contain a lot of details about implementation. Rather, it talks in global terms about the strategies the company will pursue, the benefits that will be achieved when the implementation has been completed, and how that will enable the company to move closer to achieving its fundamental purpose.

The operating plan, by contrast, is primarily intended to be a short-term guidebook (usually one year) for the executive managers and staff who have the responsibility for carrying out the plan. It contains details they need to do their work—milestones, action steps, detailed budgets and timetables, and so on. It would make dull reading for the analyst who is studying the company's strategic direction, yet its contents are essential to the manager who is charged with delivering the assigned sales goal, upgrading the computer network to Windows XP, or finding out how much money is budgeted to build the new trade show booth or hire the new engineer.

Let's look at the principal elements of a business plan, and examine how they might be treated differently in a strategic plan, as opposed to an operating plan.

Vision and Mission—The Starting Point

This is the grand purpose of the organization, the point from which everything else should emerge. There are a thousand definitions for these terms—and at least that many opinions about whether either, or both, or a "purpose statement" instead, should be the foundation for a plan. Rather than add my opinion to the pack, let me tell you what they bring to a plan. Then you decide whether a plan has adequately included them.

Vision of the Future

Any organization starts with some sort of grand purpose. Typically that grand purpose arises when the founder looks around and sees a worthwhile need that is not being filled. Abraham Lincoln had the vision of a great nation undivided by slavery. Henry Ford had the vision of a world in which almost any family could afford to own and drive an automobile. Bill Gates had the vision of a computer in every home. In each case, the vision was of the world as they thought it should be, not as it was then. Their visions seemed beyond the imagination to those around them at the time, I suspect. But then, their visions *were* beyond the imagination of normal people of their time. Their fervor, and I suspect more than a few carefully laid out plans, may explain why they were able to accomplish so much toward bringing those visions into reality. So, let's look at my definition of *vision* as I've just described it:

**Vision is the world as you define it,
arranged as you would like to see it.**

Mission—the Path to the Holy Grail

This is simpler once you understand the definition of vision:

Mission is the role of the organization in achieving the vision.

If the vision is grand enough, it is not something that one organization can achieve by itself, although it may be able to, as the visionaries above did. But as a general rule, the vision is defined and the organization then does what it can to get there.

Vision and Mission in Action—a Case Study

I had a client some years ago whose world was defined (by him) as the dental industry in Southern California. He defined his company's vision as a world (the aforementioned industry) in which hazardous waste materials from dental work would not contribute to pollution of the Southern California environment. For a variety of reasons, that world did not exist when his company was formed. Novocain, mercury, and other byproducts of dental services did not have the regulatory controls and enforcement that more visibly hazardous materials did. So it was a worthwhile purpose that was not being effectively addressed. He then went about building a company and a service that brought cost-effective hazardous materials collection and proper disposal within reach of every dentist in his world. Within a few years, his company was the dominant provider of that service throughout Southern California. He may not have achieved his mission completely, but he made great progress in that direction, and ultimately sold his company to a larger company that wanted to use his methodology to expand its own presence in that market. They in effect took over the mission he had created. And, yes, he was an excellent planner.

Strategy—Setting Direction

Once a company has decided its mission, the question likely arises: "OK, now what? How do we start? What direction do we move in?" Strategy is essentially deciding what direction the decision makers take as they begin to pursue their mission. Strategy is decided when the decision makers make an assumption about what will overcome the most significant obstacle to the vision. Abraham Lincoln had to react to the creation of the Confederate States of America; he decided the best strategy was military force, because he didn't feel the Confederate government would be convinced otherwise. Henry Ford saw how few people could afford the cars that were being built at the time; he decided he had to find a way to build a car that could be sold for $400. Bill Gates perceived that people's learning curve and resistance to technology was the prime obstacle; his strategy was to develop software that had a consistent look and feel and that would enable people to more easily use all those computers.

In each case, the decision maker assessed his market, identified the obstacle, and crafted a strategy to address the obstacle. That then sets the pattern for setting specific goals and objectives, which is a primary purpose of a business plan.

Long-Term Goals—The Path to the Mission

Up to now, the elements of the business plan have been global, intangible, and largely nonspecific. Once we move into setting goals, being specific is essential to success. In fact, setting effective goals requires attention to both the content and the structure of the goal. This is best demonstrated by an acronym that many of us have heard in one form or another at seminars and workshops on planning. The acronym is SMART and we've stretched that a bit to arrive at SMART goals, the kind that get results. Here are the characteristics of SMART goals:

Specific. The goal is identified clearly, by how much and when.

How much of the desired result constitutes success—$50,000 or five offices or 15 new employees? By when will the goal be achieved—a specific date or a specific length of time after beginning? This specificity is needed in order to ensure that everyone knows if the goal has been achieved or not. I suggest to workshop audiences that the goal is specific enough if you can be assured your 16-year-old daughter would recognize it.

Measurable. You must be able to measure the success with available data. Setting a goal to capture 20% of the market by year end is specific enough, but if there is no industry data available to measure who has what share of market, it's a meaningless goal. Set goals in areas where you can get reasonably reliable information. Bonus: it will preclude your staffers writing off the goal as smoke because they too know it can't be measured.

Achievable. The goal must be challenging, but still achievable. More to the point, it must be perceived as achievable. If the staff perceives the goal as patently unattainable, they'll give up on it from Day 1 and any efforts to reach the goal will be wasted. Goals should be set so they are a stretch beyond what exists when the goal is set, so people recognize they need to exert effort to get there, yet they should have a reasonable belief that if they really shoot for it, they can get there.

Relevant. The goal should certainly be relevant to the organization's vision, mission, and strategy. That's the whole point, after all: to get to the vision. But occasionally a manager will get excited about an opportunity that doesn't relate to the mission and will devote resources to achieve what sounds like a great idea. The problem? It takes resources and focus away from the job of the organization—fulfilling the mission.

Trackable. My word, not Webster's, but its meaning adds real substance to our goal-setting methodology. A goal is trackable if you can establish milestones to track progress toward the goal. This enables you to monitor progress and avoid unpleasant surprises at the 11th hour, when your staff "discovers" they won't make it by tomorrow, as was committed. A trackable goal might be an annual sales goal of $120,000. Seasonal adjustments aside, you might expect to bring in $10,000 a month during the year and ask

SMART Goals

Smart Managing

At any level in any organization, smart managers know that they get the best results by setting goals that are well thought out and SMART:

- **S**pecific
- **M**easurable
- **A**chievable
- **R**elevant
- **T**rackable

questions if any month fell much short of that. Thus you will know how the team is doing well before the fourth quarter and can take action to redirect resources, if necessary, to ensure the goal is met.

Short-Term Goals and Milestones—The Operating Plan

Once the grand design of the strategic plan has been laid out, the company will need a detailed plan for its managers and employees to follow. While the strategic plan typically covers a period of three to five years, its implementation is usually thought of in terms of one-year periods, each of which is guided by an annual operating plan.

The year covered by an operating plan is typically the operating or fiscal year of the company. The plan will recite the overall goals of the company for the year, then break those down into the individual goals and action items that each department must achieve or accomplish in order for the company as a whole to meet its goals. Further, for a plan to be effective, it must be trusted, meaning that employees must believe that the thought process that went into the plan had reasonable foresight, awareness, and thoroughness. Otherwise, it will be second-guessed at every step, with the likely result that every step will cost more in resources than planned, and some more challenging goals won't be met because people don't trust they can get to where the plan says they can.

The operating plan and the related budget (discussed next in Chapter 10) constitute the guidebook for action for a company's operating year. The operating plan is usually the joint effort of every department in the company, coordinated by the Finance and/or Planning Department, and each department head will have participated in the planning process by writing the goals that his or her department will achieve during the plan year. The operating plan may outline the goals and targets of each major unit within the company, the P&L budget for the year, and a budget of planned capital expenditures. In addition, subsections of the plan may be devoted to individual departments, so that each will have its individual roadmap to follow. Information included in the subsections, besides departmental goals, will likely include staffing, existing and planned additions, and the department's financial budget for the year. A suggested outline for an operating plan is shown in box starting below. This is the document that goal-driven incentive plans will typically use as their measuring stick.

Overview
  Vision, mission, strategy
  One-year summary of company goals
  Companywide challenges and opportunities

Production Department plan
  Goals
  Milestones
  Organization and staffing
  Facilities
  Challenges and opportunities
  Budget

Sales and Marketing Department plan
  Goals
  Milestones
  Organization and staffing
  Facilities

Challenges and opportunities
Budget

R&D/Product Development Department plan
Goals
Milestones
Organization and staffing
Facilities
Challenges and opportunities
Budget

Financial Department plan/budget
Goals
Milestones
Organization and staffing
Facilities
Challenges and opportunities
Budget

Companywide budget
Summary of projected basic financial statements
Departmental budgets
Departmental staffing plans
Capital expenditures plan

The layout of this outline, and even the order of its contents, is not as important as having all the bases covered. In other words, the plan should cover all these areas in a way that is logical to all people in the organization, regardless of where in the plan they appear. We have found, however, that an organization by department make it easier for each department to incorporate its contribution as well as to refer to its part of the plan during implementation or assessment of progress. The following thoughts will help you to understand what should be covered in each of these sections.

Overview

It helps to begin by reminding operating plan readers of the grand design, the overriding purpose of the company, and the direction the company is moving to fulfill that grand design.

Knowing that Wonder Widget's stated purpose was to become the dominant provider of garden equipment in the western United States helps to put in perspective the specific goals that the company wants to achieve during the upcoming year and enables every manager to buy in anew to that strategy as they begin work on the current year's goals. Whether a company decides to recite the entire vision, mission, and strategy at the beginning of the document or simply give a summary, as suggested here, is less important than the effort to reinforce the grand purpose in whatever way will succeed in gaining renewed enthusiasm for the long-term plan.

The overview should also contain the key goals the company has set for the year and the key challenges and opportunities that it will face, to keep everyone focused on the direction of the company and to keep them from getting too wrapped up in their own department agenda at the expense of the team objectives.

The Production Plan—Getting the Product Ready to Sell

Whether the company makes or buys its products or provides a service, there are activities that must be initiated and satisfactorily completed in order to have something to sell. Goals might include reaching monthly production levels that will support sale forecasts, improving machine output or maintenance downtime or setup times, or moving to just-in-time ordering to lower average inventory levels. The plan should lay these goals out, along with the timetables, staffing, and financial resources needed to achieve them.

The plan should also cover the production challenges that must be overcome in order to reach the goals and the path the organization plans to take to overcome those challenges. These might include heavy recent turnover of several skilled supervisors, the age or condition of the machines in the plan, pricing pressures from suppliers who aren't willing to provide just-in-time shipping without some price adjustments, and so on. If the plan doesn't bring these out and deal with them effectively, it will quickly become a paper tiger as employees find their paths blocked by obstacles they can't control.

Marketing and Sales Plan—Generating Interest and Making the Sale

Give the availability of the product or service, the company's sales and marketing organization (or organizations, if these are separately managed) must determine how it will interest the company's potential customers and then sell enough of its products to reach the sales goals it has set. Representative goals might include hiring and training more sales people, launching a targeted marketing campaign to raise brand awareness, introducing five new products during the year, opening and staffing three sales offices, and reducing customer complaints about product delivered vs. sales representations.

The Dilemma of the Tour Bus Industry in 2002

This client's customers are travel companies that put together vacation packages that include use of buses to transport travelers. In this segment of the travel industry, there are bus companies that own and rent out buses for holiday travel events. These bus companies have been experiencing multiple pressures on their sales as a result of three factors:

- pricing pressures from customers in a market where vacation travel is still 25% below normal due to the aftermath of 9-11
- high replacement cost for new buses combined with falling trade-in prices for their older buses, causing greater demands on their cash to periodically upgrade equipment
- dramatically rising insurance costs from insurers looking to replace loss reserves damaged by 9-11 claims.

Any bus company must address these challenges in its operating plan to have any chance of achieving the stated revenue and gross margin goals. For example, a company might offer its customers extra services that deliver high value in the customers' eyes without raising its costs too much, thus lowering the price resistance from customers. A company might also sharpen its search for better financing and hold buses a few months longer than normal, thus lowering somewhat the bus replacement cost pressures. Also, a company might shop more aggressively for insurance coverage and raise deductibles to help lower insurance costs. Perhaps the best solution might be a combination of all these options.

Challenges to be addressed might include a large competitor with a similar product, an aging product that hasn't kept up with market demands for change, strong demand for quality salespeople that keeps compensation high and candidate quality low, or pricing pressures caused by a bad economy. These challenges might be addressed by simply lowering the revenue forecast, but that indirect approach sidesteps the much more effective method of approaching each obstacle directly and identifying steps that might be taken to mitigate the potential damage.

Research & Development/Product Development Plan— Bringing New Ideas to Market

Some companies provide services that drive their sales, and continuing sales depend mostly upon delivering reliable levels of service at reasonable prices. Other companies sell products that they buy from others, usually based on the desires of their customers, and they don't create or manufacture any products. But many other companies sell proprietary products, that is, products they have developed and that they make or over which they at least maintain manufacturing control. Such products have typically been developed at some cost in time and money by these companies; that cost must be identified and reflected in their planning, along with the expected fruits of that effort in terms of new research advances, technological breakthroughs, new products developed and brought to market, and so on. For these companies, a research and development section of the operating plan is essential in order to ensure resources are allocated to these activities and to clearly set forth the expected results from use of those resources.

Their plans might identify the new products that they intend to bring to market during the coming year, based on projected outcomes of development efforts. For a drug company, for example, results might simply include a key drug moving from basic testing to first clinical trials. While the company is still years away from marketing a new product, it can still plan for and measure results in terms of progress down the development path and through the lengthy regulatory process.

Challenges are particularly great for the company engaged in research and development. For one thing, it is often impossible to know how long it will take to reach a given research goal or how much money it will cost. Unknown events or testing failures can dramatically stretch out the process, and most drug company research projects never produce a product that can be marketed and sold profitably, a situation not known when the research was begun. These companies must find a way to allocate resources, manage expectations against results, and be prepared for some good news and some bad news along the way.

Financial Plan—the Budget

This is the financial report card, the section of the plan that shows the financial results of all the work outlined in the plan. It shows the revenues that will be achieved if the sales goals are met and the expenses that will be incurred to support the sales and other goals, if everything goes according to plan. This key document will be covered in depth in Chapter 10.

Manager's Checklist for Chapter 9

❑ The term "business plan" is really a generic label. It's important to determine the purpose of the plan, its intended readership, and what is expected of its readers, in order to know the kind and depth of material that it should contain.

❑ We all plan some of our activities, but the more complex the business activities to be managed, the more important to have a plan to guide them. If a plan is needed to manage a business activity, it should be in writing, to ensure it provides clarity, a roadmap to the desired end result, consistent communication of what is to be done, and the means to empower those who will carry it out.

❑ Goals must be crafted with care to be effective in driving performance. SMART goals encompass the key characteristics that make them most likely to succeed—or at least most likely to produce a clear and mutual understanding of what was expected and what was delivered.

❑ Strategic plans are typically long-term (three to five years) and broad in their description of the goals to be achieved. Operating plans are usually short-term (one year) and more detailed in their description of the work. Strategic plans guide the operating plans. Operating plans guide the day-to-day activities that get work done.

❑ A realistic operating plan should define the goals the company wants each department to achieve and it should also outline the challenges they must overcome in order to reach the goals and how they will be met, for the plan to be both believable and achievable.

The Annual Budget: Financing Your Plans

O nce management has decided on a business plan that sets company goals for the next year, the managers need to find out (a) if they can afford to achieve those goals and (b) if the plan will make a profit for the company. Those questions are best answered by converting the operating plan's goals and actions into dollars and cents, and then breaking them down into chunks that can be evaluated and managed during daily operations. That's the purpose of the annual budget. The budget is the estimate of the financial resources that will be needed and the financial outcome of all the actions the managers will take during the budget period. It's also the financial benchmark, the report card against which their success in managing their financial resources will be measured.

The format of a typical annual budget includes a detailed, department-by-department, line-by-line estimate of the income and expenses that will occur if the operating plan is carried out as intended. It contains details sufficient to enable department managers to allocate and manage the resources allocated to them, e.g., employees, production equipment, advertising dollars, office supplies, and so forth. In fact, the bulk of the budget will look a lot like the detailed income statement from Chapter 4, with separate pages of detail for each department or division from which budget accountability is expected.

A well-prepared budget will be as detailed as necessary to track all the material sources of revenue, all significant planned expenses, and the cash flow effect of that activity. It should also include expected changes in the balance sheet as a result of the flow of money, because balance sheets are the basis for many performance measurements, as you learned in Chapter 7, and because they are also the tools used by lenders to measure compliance with loan agreement covenants. The annual budget is the focus for this chapter, because it's the most useful and most used of the financial estimating tools. However, it's not the only technique for estimating the company's financial future.

Tools for Telling the Future: Budgets, Forecasts, Projections, and Tea Leaves

There are lots of labels you may hear for financial plans. Some folks will tell you this is the "correct" name for this kind of plan or that kind of plan. But, in reality, it doesn't matter what you call it as much as what you intend to do with it. It won't matter to the owners of your company whether you call your plan a "budget" or a "forecast" or a "projection"—as long as you hit it on the money. (Of course, if you call your plan "tea leaves,"

⚠️ CAUTION!

Forecasting Rather than Planning

Forecasts are often prepared by companies that don't use annual budgets, when they find they need a tool to help them see into the immediate future. This is a risky situation, but it happens a lot in small businesses, where executives don't appreciate the value of a formal planning system, but still recognize they can't assimilate in their heads all the factors that influence their immediate financial future.

Financial plan The generic label for any kind of estimate of the future in financial terms. As such, budgets, forecasts, and projections are all financial plans. Aside from the generic usage, this term is most often used in a long-term business plan to identify the financial effects of all the activities discussed in the plan. So, in Chapter 9 we referred to the dollars-and-cents representation of our long-range plan as a financial plan. The resulting definition: an integrated, multiyear plan of income, expenses, cash flow, and balance sheet changes.

Projection Estimate that is less detailed than a financial plan and usually covers a shorter period of time, typically prepared to demonstrate expected financial results over a few months or a year, perhaps for a special purpose such as a bank loan or to test the continuing validity of a budget or long-range plan. It may not include an integrated balance sheet, but it will almost always include a P&L projection or a cash flow projection, depending on the focus.

Forecast Typically a very short-term view of the next few weeks or months, perhaps to use to test the validity of the operating budget under a set of conditions that might not have existed when the annual budget was created. Short-term cash forecasts are typically not very detailed. A forecast might also be used as the starting point in budgeting, such as producing a sales forecast that will form the basis for the sales budget.

you may have a credibility problem, even with great results.) Most of these variations differ principally in the level of detail they contain, the depth of work that went into their preparation, and the period of time they cover. Still, it's worthwhile to know the most common usage, if for no other reason than because these are the definitions we are using in this book.

How to Budget for Revenues—the "Unpredictable" Starting Point

Every budget preparation cycle should begin with a revenue forecast. This is so for very valid reasons. Revenue typically drives the business and determines the level of growth and the degree of success that the business may anticipate. The level of revenue determines the magnitude of investment that management can make in the business and the amount of resources that it may purchase to run the business.

For many managers, this is a frustrating way to begin. Not only must they take the time to prepare a budget, but they have to start with the one thing they can neither control nor accurately predict—the amount of products and services their customers will buy from them during the budget period. Still, that's how it's done, except in the smallest of companies, companies with aging owners who have become highly risk-averse, or some professional service firms where the primary focus is on covering their fixed costs. Such narrowly focused thinking is not consistent with building a successful, forward-looking company, but for some it represents protecting what they have, a primary concern.

If we accept the value of beginning with a sales forecast, the very next question is usually "How do we do it?" How

Let the Salespeople Do It, Henry!

Smart Managing Whatever the structure of the company, the sales forecast should come from the people who are directly responsible for bringing in the sales, the company's sales force. While top management may feel it's important to announce their sales desires, hopes, and expectations, it's a very risky business to build those goals into the company budget without the validation of the people who actually sell the goods or services. Salespeople know the market better than anyone else, typically, and they know what customers want and don't want, even if they don't always communicate it effectively to management. Besides, they must buy into the sales budget, just as any employees should take personal responsibility for any goal assigned to them. Otherwise, they may well consider it "management's budget" and not theirs. The result is often failure to achieve the plan.

This approach has some risks, however. Salespeople may want to set less aggressive sales goals because they don't want to be evaluated against target they're not sure they can hit. Also, if your salespeople are primarily outside sales representatives rather than employees, their sense of your market and their commitment to the company may influence the care with which they prepare their estimates. These risks do not, however, lessen the importance of having the salespeople adopt the sales forecast as their own.

to budget for revenues depends in large measure on the nature of the business, its history, and the buying patterns of its customers. Figure 10-1 shows some ideas and the kinds of businesses for which they might make sense.

Sales Scenario	Ideas for Estimating Annual Revenues
1. The company sells its products to an identifiable list of customers and there are good relationships between Sales and the customers.	Identify the top 50 (or X) customers representing 60% or more of the company's business and contact them for their buying intentions for the coming year. Include an estimate for the remainder, based on the trends seen in the first group.
2. The historical sales pattern has closely followed some indicator of growth that's still available and still reasonably valid, e.g., airline passenger miles, housing starts, auto sales, defense spending, personal income statistics, etc.	Obtain the most valid forecast of that indicator for the coming year and base the sales estimate on the same relationship that has existed in the past year. If the relationship has changed over the years, weigh the most recent periods most heavily in your estimates.
3. The company has been able to sell all it can make in a strong market and it's feeling the pinch of reaching its productive capacity.	Project sales as a percent of maximum capacity to produce, recognizing that 100% is not attainable, but that capacity will strongly affect a company's ability to deliver. In this case, the production managers should also be part of the estimating team.
4. Customers perform work under long-term contracts with their customers, so they must line up supplier commitments to enable them to project profitability on their performance.	Similar to 1 above, except that the estimates are likely to be more reliable. Still, history tells us even these are uncertain, as delays by others can cause postponement or even cancellation. This is, after all, still just an estimate.
5. Sales have grown at a rate that has been reasonably consistent from year to year and nothing in the market is expected to change.	This is the no-brainer estimate, providing nothing is expected to change in the coming year. Use the same growth rate, perhaps increased by whatever the company's managers think they can do to boost results further.

Figure 10-1. Estimating Revenues

Once finished, the sales estimate will be presented to management, who will evaluate its viability in terms of the following:

- A reasonable balance between aggressiveness and conservatism. Did the sales manager push for a little more than was attainable easily without creating expectations that no one can reasonably meet?
- The likely acceptance of the estimate by the salespeople, balanced against the ability of the company to make an acceptable profit if the estimate were adopted and met.
- The abilities and resources available to the production side of the company to deliver the goods and services outlined in the estimate.

If the sales estimate is deemed acceptable, it will become the sales budget for the company. All other budgets will then have to take into account the resources they'll need to support the sales budget. If it's not yet acceptable, it likely means a back-and-forth process of questioning, additional research, and negotiating between management and the sales organization until an acceptable revenue budget is adopted.

Budgeting Costs—Understanding Relationships That Affect Costs

Budgeting, in its simplest form, is an attempt to estimate what will happen to a company's financial condition if it sells a certain quantity of goods and services and runs its business in support of that sales record. Managers want to know what they will have to spend in order to sell the quantities they have budgeted and exactly what they will spend it for. This sounds simple enough—except for this principle, perhaps an obscure extension of Parkinson's Law:

There is always a good reason to spend money.

As Parkinson might have said it, the need for money expands to consume all the available funds. In other words, there's always a logical reason to approve a given expenditure. Every department needs more resources to do its job—or at least that case can always be made and apparently supported. Most companies today are trying to get by with lower costs than previously, as a hedge against the possibility that sales or profits will be lower than planned. Whether an expenditure will deliver the expected benefit or not is a big question, of course, but a manager can't know the answer until he or she makes the expenditure, so it's hard to disapprove an expenditure in advance unless it violates some predetermined standard, like a budget.

Given that premise, managers can choose to accept every rationale extended by an employee that seems logical, or they can audit the validity of every request to spend money, or they can simply make arbitrary choices until they run out of money. Since none of those options is wise in today's business environment, senior managers must find a way to relate the need to spend money to what's really needed to support their sales goals, their R&D goals, their expansion goals, or whatever their operating plan calls for as the measure of success for the coming year.

Enter the budget—a planning and analysis tool that enables management to estimate the expenditures needed to support a given level of sales and to set spending limits based on those estimates. Remember that some expenses are variable with sales, some are fixed, and some are somewhere between variable and fixed (semi-fixed). You can begin to see the possibility that we can create a budget that documents those relationships and thus sets limits on reasonable spending for potentially every item in the company's chart of accounts.

We already know that variable costs grow or shrink in direct relation to sales levels. If you think about it, though, many other cost items in a budget have identifiable relationships to other cost items, not just sales. Those relationships can enable a company to base its spending decisions on its own operating history.

For example, assume that last year group medical insurance

cost the company 2% of wages paid and the insurer has announced a 10% rate increase for the coming year. It then makes sense to build a budget that includes health insurance at 2.2% of budgeted labor costs for next year (10% more than last year's 2%), with the comfort that the relationship will hold at almost any labor level. Now the company doesn't have to reconsider health care costs with every budget revision. It can simply let budgeted health insurance costs follow budgeted wages, which are controllable.

Figure 10-2 shows some relationships that may help a company develop a budget with built-in controls on costs that might otherwise be difficult to estimate, based on their relationship to other costs that are more visible.

You can probably think of more of these relationships that would apply to your company's budget, but this will give you an idea of the possibilities. Keep in mind that a line item that's budgeted based on a percent of sales, when the activity bears no relation to sales, is a waste of time as a control tool. That becomes calculation without accuracy and without value, other than to fill a space in the budget file. Look for the relationships that have meaning, even if the basis for a predominantly fixed cost is simply last year's actual expense plus an inflation factor, as it sometimes might be, such as when budgeting for building rent.

The Budgeting Process—Trial and Error

So you've exerted diligent effort, honestly given your department's budget your best sense of accuracy, and provided for every cost you think might be incurred to meet the goals you've been assigned. You feel confident as you send your budget to your boss. (You're the first of her direct reports to get yours in—another feather in your cap.) You wait for the feedback after all the other departments submit their parts and all the departments, divisions, and cost centers get combined into a total company draft plan.

This line item to be budgeted	... may be assumed to change in relation to
Sales commissions	Sales volume, especially if segmented by products commissioned at differing rates
Payroll taxes, health insurance, and workers' compensation insurance	Wages and salaries
Auto expenses	Number of employees reimbursed for such expenses
Selling expenses	Sales volume (in units, if available)
Telephone expense	Number of employees with offices and phones
Plant supervision wages	Number of employees with that job title
Factory janitorial services, outsourced	Square feet of factory space serviced
Profit-sharing expense	Wages and salaries of eligible employees
Travel expense	Number of employee travel days planned*
Sales taxes	Taxable sales
Utilities	Square feet of space occupied (plant vs. office)
Property taxes	Square feet of space occupied
Building repairs and maintenance	Square feet of space occupied
Machine repairs and maintenance	Machine hours in use or available
Telephone expense in the sales department	Number of full-time-equivalent salespeople

*This can be further refined by intrastate, national, and international travel days.

Figure 10-2. Cost relationships that facilitate sound budgeting

Imagine how you'd feel if the next thing you heard was your manager telling you that you need to cut 10% from your budget, without any reduction in the goals for which you will be held accountable. If you've been in the corporate world for very long, you know this is fairly common. But why? If everyone else did his or her part as diligently as you, this wouldn't happen, would it?

Well, actually, it might.

The process of producing a company-wide budget involves various departments estimating the resources they feel they will need to meet their goals—sales targets, customer service response rates, launch of new products or services, marketing department development of new collateral materials for trade shows, etc. No one knows what the total of all those cost budgets will be until they're added together. Only then can the top managers get the first sense of whether or not their overall sales and profit goals are likely to be met by the combined budget submissions. If they do, approval is all that's necessary to make the draft the new, official budget. But more often they don't.

So, in fulfilling their responsibilities to the owners or stockholders, management must ask everyone to re-look at his or her proposals and find ways to raise revenues (again) or reduce expenses in order to improve the budgeted bottom line. This is exactly the back-and-forth process that occurred earlier with the revenue budget. The objective is to achieve a happy medium in which top management is content with the sale and profit commitments of the organization and managers with budget responsibility are comfortable that they can achieve the assigned goals with the budgeted resources.

During such reassessment, managers might look to ideas such as these to reevaluate their cost requests:

- Operating with the minimum number of employees that can handle the work
- Better worker training to improve productivity and reduce turnover
- Reducing plan operating costs, such as by using automation to save on labor costs
- A lease vs. buy analysis before acquiring new equipment (note that this also has cash flow ramifications, another consideration for growing companies)

- Negotiating better prices and terms with suppliers and developing alternate suppliers
- Planning more use of overtime to reduce the need to hire more permanent workers (although there's a cost in terms of overtime premium that reduces the savings from this option)
- Modifying planned sales and marketing campaigns where results are not reasonably ensured
- Changing distribution methods, combining delivery routes, reducing smaller orders, and so on

In a company where budget decisions are controlled by top management, the negotiation process may indeed be simply an edict to "cut 10%" from every department. In 1967, when Ronald Reagan became governor of California, he created a huge furor when he did exactly that in trying to balance the state's budget. He soon relented and found a more objective way to reduce costs. But the lesson was still lost on many corporate managers, perhaps because an across-the-board cut avoids making hard, individual decisions.

In a more empowering management environment, top management will ask subordinates to remove more cost from less critical functions and less from the more critical departments.

Hard Lessons Learned the Easy Way

Upper-level managers who mandate cutting a certain percentage across all departments may do more than create a furor; they can also cause severe and lasting damage. What does a savvy manager do who anticipates an order to reduce by 5% across the board? He or she raises all figures by 5%. So management gains nothing—unless it orders a 10% reduction. And a savvy manager who is unsure about the percentage to be applied would likely pad the budget for a worst-case scenario.

The result is that the managers are playing cat-and-mouse "negotiation" games with the figures—a lot of time and effort wasted simply because upper management prefers making budget cuts "the easy way." Good managers make hard, individual budget decisions for the good of the company.

This process takes longer and involves more back-and-forth, trial-and-error manipulation of the numbers. But it will usually result in a more equitable budget that's easier for subordinates to buy into, rather than the alternative—acceptance of the edict from above, all the while holding the quiet belief that "it will take a lot of luck to make these numbers."

Flexible Budgets—Whatever Happens, We've Got a Budget for It

One of the most useful tools in the manufacturing environment, and in many other kinds of companies as well, is the *flexible budget*. This tool is an extension of the classic budgeting methodology that is most valuable when these two statements are both true:

1. The company expects or may experience wide variations in levels of activity within some area of the company, such as sales.
2. Many of the costs vary directly with those levels of activity, e.g., they are direct costs tied to sales, and the budget controls for these costs would be marginally useless if activity levels were significantly different from those in the budget.

Key Term

Flexible budget A set of projections of revenue and expenses at various levels of production or sales. A flexible budget, because it's based upon different levels of activity, is very useful for comparing actual costs experienced with the costs allowed for the activity level achieved. A series of budgets can be readily developed to fit any activity level.

In this situation, it's wise to develop a flexible budget, in which directly related costs are budgeted for various levels of activity and the budget used for comparison with actual results is the budget that's based on the actual activity levels achieved.

How does a flexible budget work? Let's assume The Wonder Widget Company is projecting production of its WW-1000 at

500 units a month, but with inefficiency, unexpected problems, or perhaps even good luck, volume could be anywhere from 300 units to 600 units, a big variation for which to plan. Such fluctuations could significantly impair budget analysis. Looking at the internal reports, we see that production numbers for the month of July came out as shown in Figure 10-3.

Item	Units	Actual Costs
Budgeted production	500 units	
Actual production	400 units	
Direct labor		$28,500
Variable overhead		$64,000
Total variable costs		*$92,500*

Figure 10-3. Wonder Widget production statistics for July 2003

Production in this example fell well short of the amount budgeted, with the result that variable costs, which fluctuate based on the amount produced, were lower than planned. A budget variance report using a static budget—one based solely on a single, planned level of activity—might look like Figure 10-4.

On this basis, the production department looks like it did pretty well, because it beat budget by $15,000. However, it was only 80% successful at meeting production expectations. So, how efficient was it?

If we look at the same facts under a flexible budget system, we get a different and more accurate picture in terms of success in meeting company goals. In this case,

> **Budget variance report**
> A financial report usually prepared for each department or unit that is operating under a budget authorization, which is used to summarize the actual revenues earned and costs incurred, compared with the budgeted revenues and costs, and to present the variance between the two. Such reports are usually prepared showing monthly and year-to-date comparative results.

	Actual cost per unit produced	Budget cost per unit produced	Actual	Static Budget	Variance: Favorable (Unfavorable)
Production in units			400	500	(100)
Direct labor	$71.25	$65.00	$28,500	$32,500	$4,000
Variable overhead	$160.00	$150.00	64,000	75,000	11,000
Total variable costs			**$92,500**	**$107,500**	**$15,000**

Figure 10-4. Wonder Widget variance report using a static budget

we use a budget based on the volume of activity and a cost-volume formula that enables us to produce a budget tailored to the level of activity. Figure 10-5 shows the result.

The combination of the under-plan production and the use of a flexible budget convey a very different and more informative picture (Figure 10-5).

	Actual cost per unit produced	Budget cost per unit produced	Actual	Flexible Budget	Variance: Favorable (Unfavorable)
Production in units			400	400	—
Direct labor	$71.25	$65.00	$28,500	$26,000	$(2,500)
Variable overhead	$160.00	$150.00	64,000	60,000	(4,000)
Total variable costs			**$92,500**	**$86,000**	**$(6,500)**

Figure 10-5. Wonder Widget variance report using a flexible budget

As you can see, the production department's efficiency is better measured with the flexible budget, which shows it actually *exceeded* the budget by $6,500 for the level of results it delivered. That information might be lost if a static budget is used. That's why flexible budgets are smart when management wants to create a budget that does not reward the underspending that typically accompanies underproduction.

While flexible budgeting (or "flex" budgeting, as the "in crowd" refers to it) is more effort to prepare, it's much more effective in the right circumstances. Of course, the reverse is

> ### Inefficiency Can Cost Money in Many Ways
>
> If you look closely at Figure 10-4 and if you were to calculate unit costs for budgeted production vs. actual production, you would notice that the budgeted unit labor cost was $65 per unit ($32,500/500) but the actual labor cost came out to $71.25 per unit ($28,500/400). How can that be when the costs vary with production quantities? The answer is that labor is inefficient when it doesn't function at the levels for which the workforce was designed. The labor force in this case didn't use its time efficiently, but still got paid for the time spent, with the result that the actual direct labor cost incurred was more per unit than budgeted.
>
> Looking at the variable overhead, a similar situation exists. Budgeted overhead per unit was $150, but actual overhead was $160. Since overhead allocation typically follows labor cost, this increase results from allocating overhead to the inefficient labor that was charged but didn't produce anything.

also true. If conditions do not vary greatly, such as in an administrative department with largely fixed costs, a flex budget would simply be a lot more work and provide very little benefit.

Variance Reporting and Taking Action

In Chapter 8 we explored variances from standard manufacturing cost and how they help us identify and correct production inefficiencies. In the manufacturing environment, standard cost is the budget, in effect, for making a single unit of product. Nonmanufacturing companies and the other departments in a manufacturing company don't use standard costs, per se, but they use budgets, and variance analysis serves the same purpose for them as for the plant.

Variance reporting is a variation on the traditional management concept of *management by exception,* as defined in Chapter 8. The purpose of variance reporting is to enable managers to be more time-efficient in locating and correcting problems by creating reports that focus primarily on the problems, or exceptions. So the report is laid out to calculate and highlight differences between actual costs and budgeted costs. Figure

The Wonder Widget Company
Budget Variance Report, Sales, July 2003

	Current Month			Year to Date		
	Actual	**Budget**	**Variance**	**Actual**	**Budget**	**Variance**
Salaries	$42,050	$40,920	$(1,130)	$294,500	$287,000	$(7,500)
Payroll taxes	4,420	4,092	(328)	29,920	28,700	(1,220)
Workers' comp	575	409	(166)	3,010	2,870	(140)
Group insurance	1,550	1,200	(350)	15,200	8,500	(6,700)
Advertising	3,250	1,976	(1,274)	42,005	45,000	2,995
Automobile	800	650	(150)	5,520	4,800	(720)
Business promotion	950	1,050	100	7,260	7,500	240
Commissions	1,520	1,478	(42)	11,650	10,500	(1,150)
Meals and entertainment	475	560	85	4,250	3,600	(650)
Insurance	675	642	(33)	2,650	4,300	1,650
Office supplies	250	200	(50)	1,675	1,400	(275)
Outside services	810	1,000	190	8,210	7,200	(1,010)
Postage	275	300	25	2,246	2,500	254
Rent	11,500	11,500	—	80,500	80,500	—
Telephone	400	450	50	3,350	3,200	(150)
Trade shows	5,450	5,000	(450)	18,450	25,000	6,550
Travel and lodging	3,695	3,500	(195)	17,320	18,000	680
Total Sales/Marketing	**$78,645**	**$74,927**	**$(3,718)**	**$547,716**	**$540,570**	**$(7,146)**

Figure 10-6. Wonder Widget budget variance report (sales)

10-6 shows an example of such a report for the sales department of Wonder Widget.

Numbers in variance columns are in parentheses if unfavorable. The format is designed to facilitate quick review and recognition of the numbers that are out of bounds or over budget. Some reports might also include columns for variance percent, to show each variance as a percentage of the budget for that line item. Again, the idea is to easily identify the significant differences so that management can move immediately to corrective action. A report such as this should be prepared every month for every department in the company, as well as for the company as a whole, to help top management meet its profit goals.

Three Magic Questions for Variance Control
A department manager should look at his or her variance report each month and ask these three questions:

1. Why did this variance occur? What happened that caused the amount we spent to be materially different from what we intended to spend? "We bought more office supplies." Wrong. "We bought more office supplies to avoid a large, just announced price increase." Right.

2. What action must I take now, immediately, to keep a negative variance from continuing or to try to keep a positive variance from slipping away?

3. What am I learning from the answers to the first two questions that will make my budget next year a more effective management tool?

These short questions are very powerful and useful for two important reasons:

- They will help the manager to move quickly from analysis to action.
- The manager's boss is likely to ask the same questions, one way or another, and it's useful to have the answers in advance, if the manager is career-minded—or even just interested in surviving.

Manager's Checklist for Chapter 10

❏ Every budget development cycle should begin with an estimate of the revenues the company can expect to earn. While this may first be announced as a management goal, it's critical for the sales department to accept as its own whatever sales budget is adopted. That usually occurs when it is directly involved in the revenue budget development process.

❏ There's always a good reason to spend money. Budget developers and approvers must always keep in mind the operating goals of the company for the period under review and not allow a "good reason" to permit a budgeted expenditure that's not in the best interests of meeting the company's goals.

❏ The budget preparation process is a trial-and-error process, because we're bringing together information from diverse sources to work toward a company goal. The chances of hitting that target on the first try are slim, so managers should simply expect to rework the budget at least once and accept the frustration of repeating their efforts, because a good budget is worth the work.

❏ Flexible budgets are an excellent tool for organizations with outcomes and costs that can vary widely. They are used when management wants to create a budget that does not reward the underspending that typically accompanies underproduction. A flexible budget enables adjustment of cost budgets to the level that would be expected at various levels of productivity, thus permitting measurement of efficiency at the actual level of activity.

❏ Remember the three magic questions for getting the most benefit from budget variance reports:
  • Why did it happen?
  • What immediate action should we take?
  • What are we learning that will make the next budget a better management tool?

Financing the Business

Financing the Business:

Understanding the Debt vs. Equity Options

Throughout this book we have referred to the investment in a business that provides the cash for the business to get started and begin operations. We've also looked at a balance sheet that showed debt owed by the business—money borrowed for some corporate purpose. But we have yet to talk about how the money was raised and how the debt or equity got onto the books.

How a Business Gets Financed—In the Beginning and Over Time

While there are many books on this subject alone, we need to get an overview of this important area. As we come to the final chapters in this book, we will look at both debt and equity financing, what they are, how they work, and why an owner or CEO might choose one or the other, or both, to meet the company's financing needs.

A word about competition: lending is a very competitive

business, particularly among commercial banks. Large banks and small banks are competing for your business, just like the TV ads proclaim. Every bank offers a range of borrowing options. Even though banks pay similar rates for the money they receive in deposits and federal loans, they often have different needs in terms of the kinds of loans they want on their books. Bank A may have only 40% home mortgage loans when its target is 50%, so it will likely offer very favorable rates to attract more home mortgage borrowers. Bank B may have done that already and now be up to its goal with mortgage loans but behind target on construction loans, so it will offer favorable financing to builders to bring in more of that kind of business. Thus their respective home mortgage rates may be quite different, even though they both pay the same rates for their money. It pays to shop around, whether you are an individual, a small business, or a mega corporation.

A company obtains working capital either by selling a portion of the company to investors (equity)—which we'll discuss in Chapter 12—or by getting a loan from a bank or other lending source (debt). There are seemingly endless variations of debt, from basic forms of borrowing that we'll discuss in this chapter to more exotic borrowing options that are beyond the scope of this book.

The principal common attribute of all these forms of debt is that they require repayment at some point, unlike equity financing, which involves the permanent sale of a share of ownership. That seems simple enough—but there are exceptions: *convertible* debt may be exchanged for equity and not repaid, under certain circumstances, and sometimes equity ownership in an emerging company carries a condition that the company may repurchase it, again under certain circumstances.

That said, let's look at the principal kinds of debt, those you will likely encounter most of the time, and not concern ourselves with the unusual exceptions.

Short-Term Debt—Balancing Working Capital Needs

Every company has short-term debt of one kind or another, obligations that it must repay sometime in the next 12 months. Its purpose is to extend the working capital resources of the company and to put more money to work earning for the company, so the owners don't need to put more cash into the company's bank account. It includes both short-term borrowing from the bank and traditional trade credit.

The most common kind is trade credit—accounts payable to suppliers, typically extended for 30 days at a time and without formal loan agreements. However, many companies also have formal arrangements to obtain additional short-term debt in the form of loans from banks or other lenders. Here are some examples of needs for working capital that may be relieved by short-term borrowing:

- increasing accounts receivable balances, perhaps to finance rapidly growing sales on credit or a slowdown in receiving payment of open customer balances,
- inventory buildups due to a planned new product introduction, preparation for a heavy selling season, or avoidance of an upcoming supplier price increase,
- a temporary cash shortage caused by operating losses the company has incurred but expects to recover from soon, as long as it can rebuild its working capital in the interim, or
- a business cycle that inherently includes alternating periods of negative cash flow (to manufacture) and positive cash flow (to sell).

Some examples will serve to show the variety that is possible here.

Revolving Credit Line

A revolving credit line is a promise by a bank (typically) or other lender to provide cash on demand up to a certain maximum, the credit limit. The borrower obtains a revolving credit line based on

TRICKS OF THE TRADE

Use Short-Term Debt Only for Short-Term Needs

Business owners squeezed for cash to expand sometimes make a big mistake. Because short-term financing is often easier to get than long-term financing, they borrow short-term money, then renew or stretch out their repayment, using the money to satisfy long-term needs such as multi-year marketing programs, new product development and introduction, and so on. If the long-term plans take longer to bear fruit than they had expected, the businesses may be strained for cash to repay short-term debt that can no longer be delayed and their working capital can be badly damaged.

The key: use *short-term* debt for working capital that will generate the funds to repay the loan in accordance with its terms and use *long-term* debt to finance long lead-time projects for which the timing of a return is uncertain.

its projected need for short-term cash and its available collateral. The company then borrows—or draws against the line—as it needs the cash and repays it when the need is gone. Thus, the actual borrowing fluctuates over time and the cash advanced by the bank revolves: in other words, it's borrowed, repaid, and then borrowed again, as the creditor's cash needs change. The lender will typically charge a variable rate for the amount outstanding and may charge other credit line fees as well.

Key Term

Revolving credit line An agreement by a bank or other lender to lend cash on demand up to a specified limit and then, as the borrower pays back all or part of the loan, to allow the borrower to borrow up to that limit again, as often as needed. Also known as a *revolver*.

Revolving credit lines may be collateralized by liens on the company's assets, such as accounts receivable, inventories, equipment, or property. Typically a lender will extend credit up to 70% to 90% of eligible receivables and perhaps 50% to 70% of eligible inventories. These credit lines may also be unsecured for the financially strongest customers of the lender. Most companies with short-term credit needs will try to satisfy their needs by using revolving credit lines, because these lines enable them to obtain cash when they need it and to limit their interest expense when they don't.

Revolving credit lines are widely used to meet temporary working capital needs. Such lines provide easy and flexible borrowing and allow a company to control borrowing costs.

> **Collateral** Assets pledged by a borrower to protect the interests of the lender by guaranteeing the repayment of the loan. A loan is *collateralized* or *secured* by the assets pledged. Typically, the lender will want the collateral to exceed the amount of the loan, to ensure that, in the event of default, it has some cushion in disposing of the collateral and getting full payment of its loan.

Loans are for working capital purposes and can be used for any business purpose, as long as the borrowings are protected by adequate collateral.

Accounts Receivable Loans—Collecting Before You Collect

Companies that don't have the cash to finance their operations while waiting for their customers to pay them and companies that have the cash but want to use it for other purposes may borrow money from a bank or other lender and pledge their accounts receivable as collateral for the loan. This is a simpler variation of the revolving credit line, in that the lender will make advances up to a certain percentage of eligible receivables, with the general expectation that the company will repay the line when it collects the accounts. Terms and conditions vary widely, including what is eligible, what constitutes a good credit risk, how quickly advances must be repaid, and so on. Just like the revolver, advances against receivables enable the company to retain control of its collection activities and its credit risk (unlike *factoring*, discussed below, in which both of control and risk often—but not always—pass to the lender).

Accounts receivable lending works very much like the revolver, except that accounts receivable are the only assets used to calculate how much may be borrowed. Advances are pretty much limited to 70% to 90% of the value of the eligible collateral. Depending on the lender, there may be monthly or quarterly reporting of statistics and quarterly or annual audits by bank accountants to satisfy the lender that the company is properly handling its paperwork and collection activities. Borrowing cost for such loans is best characterized as medium—not the lowest rates and not the highest. Actual rates depend very much on the lender's credit policies, the creditworthiness of the borrower, and the relationship between them. Yes, even though these are considered collateral loans, the lender's willingness to lend and flexibility on terms and conditions are very much influenced by the relationship between borrower and lender.

Factoring—Selling Accounts Receivable and Passing Along the Risk (Sometimes)

For companies whose credit rating is not strong enough to warrant other forms of borrowing, there is the option of factoring, or selling the company's accounts receivable balances for immediate cash. This is a widely used but relatively high-cost option—typically from 15% to 30% percent APR—so companies typically won't choose this source if another option is available to them.

Here's how it works. A factoring company, or "factor," will purchase the customer invoices individually, following a detailed review to identify accounts and invoices that qualify. The factor pays the company for each invoice, after deducting a discount, usually 3% to 5% of the amount of the invoice. The discount compensates the factor for two things: (a) interest on the money from the time it is paid until the customer repays them, and (b) a premium for assuming the risk of collection from the company. The company then will typically notify their customer that the invoice owed to the company should now be paid to the factor, rather than the company. When the customer pays in due course, the factor receives 100% of the balance due, and thus gets their money back, plus their fees. Along with this process is a relatively heavy paperwork load in selling individual invoices, documents flowing back and forth often daily—from the borrower to support amounts sold, and from the factor to document amounts collected, advanced, charged back under recourse agreements and so on.

Besides their fees and account-by-account scrutiny, the factor may build in additional safeguards against loss. It may, for

> **Factoring** The selling of a company's accounts receivable at a discount to a business (a *factor*) that assumes the credit risk of the accounts and receives cash as the debtors pay off their accounts. Also known as *accounts receivable financing.*

Key Term

example, purchase invoices "with recourse," meaning it has the right to sell the invoices back to the borrower if it has not collected from the customer within a certain time, thus protecting the factor from a loss of principal. There may also be other fees and restrictions that effectively increase the cost of the loan even more.

Don't Let Interest Costs Eat the Company's Lunch

CAUTION!

Factoring is a good example of borrowing that is costly enough that it can adversely affect profitability if not used with care, especially by companies with marginal profits. For example, a cash-strapped company with a hot product may feel it makes sense to pay a factor to get early access to cash so it can continue to expand sales. But factoring charges add up fast.

Let's suppose a company factors $1.2 million of sales under a plan that charges 4% per invoice (a mid-range price) and customer balances are outstanding for two months on average. That means the company borrows, repays, and re-borrows $200,000 six times a year, paying $8,000 in fees each time ($200,000 x 4%). In a year, the company pays $48,000 in factoring fees ($8,000 x 6)—but has the use of *only $200,000* of the factor's money at any one time. That's an *effective interest rate of 24%!* If the company nets 10% pretax profit from sales, its pretax profit of $120,000 has been cut by *40%* to gain access to that cash.

Factoring may be a good decision, but only in special circumstances. Managers should do their homework before choosing this option— and any decision to use factoring for financing should come with a plan to systematically remove the need in the future.

Certain kinds of companies use factoring as a normal business tool, perhaps because they have not been sufficiently well financed from the beginning or because margins are so thin that they have been unable to earn enough profits to build a working capital base. The U.S. garment industry, populated by many small, creatively driven businesses, is an example.

Honorable Mention to Some Other Short-Term Borrowing Techniques

Flooring—buying inventory without paying for it until it's sold. This is a little like consignment buying, commonly used years ago to induce retailers to carry products they didn't want to pay for until they sold. The difference? Flooring is a financing method for high-ticket items like cars and boats. Dealers cannot typically afford to pay for a showroom full of inventory, so they borrow against the inventory, item by item, and pay off the loan when they sell the item. They pay the lender—such as GE Capital, a bank, or a finance company—interest (the "flooring charge") based on how long they held the item on their premises. Financing plans can include only inventory or a combination of inventory and receivables.

Inventory financing. This is another way to use inventory as collateral. It's possible to obtain financing using the inventory a company owns as collateral, but it isn't easy. It must be possible to sell the inventory readily if necessary, which means that only certain kinds of raw materials and finished goods will qualify. Even then, the loan amount will be limited to 50% or so of the inventory value and the lender will often want additional collateral as well. Inventory can be hard to liquidate if the borrower defaults on the loan, so the lender has greater risk of loss; constraints on inventory lending limit the lender's potential losses. There isn't much of this kind of lending today.

Purchase order financing. This is going factoring one step better—or worse. A company that wins a large customer order that it doesn't have the cash to fulfill can borrow money on the strength of the purchase order to enable it to manufacture the products needed to fill the order. This is very high-risk lending, because the lender is betting the borrower will be able to make the product and successfully deliver it. As a result, the requirements for this kind of borrowing are even stricter than for factoring: strong customer, firm purchase order, borrower with good track record of completing its work, and so on. Only the smallest companies with the weakest working capital position, or those with unusually large, one-time orders, typically seek this kind of financing.

Long-Term Debt—Semi-Permanent Capital or Asset Acquisition Financing

Let's now look at the benefits of taking on long-term debt as yet another way a business can finance itself.

Term Loans—the Old-Fashioned Way

A term loan is the kind of loan you and I use to purchase real estate or to finance that dream vacation. We borrow the money, use it for its intended purpose, and repay it in installments over several years.

How does it work? To get such a loan, a company will apply to its bank or other lender. Upon approval, the bank advances the money and the company signs documents promising to repay the loan over some number of years in monthly installments, including principal and interest. The bank will usually require the pledge of collateral to make the loan, which might include a specific asset or it might be all assets of the company that are not already encumbered with debt. If the loan is for real estate, the real estate will always be pledged as collateral for the loan. If the company is privately held, collateral might also include a personal guarantee by the owners. Interest costs for such a loan are typically moderate, as a company must be in reasonably sound financial condition to be approved. Such borrowers are in demand and banks will often compete for the business of solid business borrowers.

Who uses it? A company might use a term loan to finance an acquisition program, to develop or improve new products for its market, or to obtain funds to buy or build a factory. The idea is to put a large amount of money to work immediately and repay it over time as the company receives the benefits of the front-end investment. The company expects that the additional earnings or other benefits will more than cover the cost of servicing the debt, including principal and interest, for the life of the loan and hopefully beyond. The challenge for many companies is to do a thorough enough analysis that the return is reasonably assured before they take on the long-term debt obligation. The risk is that a company won't be able to pay off the loan, which means a painful series of meetings and negotiations with the lenders as everyone tries to work out a win-win solution to the dilemma. This is the stuff of which corporate turnarounds are made.

Equipment Purchasing or Leasing—Two Paths to One Goal

Equipment purchasing is what you do when you buy a new car. You pick the car, negotiate the loan, and buy the car and the bank pays the seller off. Then you make installment payments to the lender until you've paid off the loan and you finally own the car. In exactly the same manner, a company can buy manufacturing equipment or computers or, for that matter, new cars. The business purpose is to extend the outlay of cash for the new equipment over a period of time more closely related to the length of time the purchase is providing benefit to the company.

Such loans are typically paid off in three to five years, well before the equipment is worn out, so the benefit continues after the loan is paid and the strain on the company's cash balances is minimized. This is particularly valuable to rapidly growing companies that, as we've noted earlier, have a constant appetite for cash to finance their growth. The cost of such loans is typically related to the creditworthiness of the borrower and the expected value of the collateral over the life of the loan. Interest rates charged will vary, but will be higher than loans secured by stable collateral and lower than loans with greater risk, like factoring.

Payments are structured to provide principal and interest with a level payment each month. That means, of course, that earlier payments are mostly interest with little principal reduction. (Have you ever looked at your home loan statements a year or so after buying or refinancing? You're not paying much principal, are you?) The level payment makes repayment manageable for the borrower, but the downside is the low rate of principal reduction until late in the life of the loan. One option: shorten the life of the loan. Principal reduction is increased in shorter-term loans and interest cost is correspondingly decreased.

A variation on the equipment purchase loan is the equipment lease. The cash management objective is the same, but the money is often easier to find because the lender/lessor has a stronger hold on the collateral until the company has paid the full amount of the loan. In an equipment purchase, the lender has a lien on the equipment, but the borrower actually owns the equipment. Thus, legal action in the event of default is somewhat involved. By contrast, under a lease agreement, the equipment lessor, not the borrower, owns the equipment. The lessor remains the legal owner until the lease obligation has been satisfied in full and the lessee either purchases the asset or returns it to the lessor. Collection action is simpler in event of default. Risk is less, making a lease often easier to obtain than a purchase loan.

The cost of equipment leasing will typically be higher than the cost of an equipment purchase loan, if for no other reason than there's usually an intermediary (the lessor) between the buyer and the seller. This cost comparison rule-of-thumb is not always valid because there are other considerations that affect cost. Tax benefits that can accrue to a lessor who continues to own the equipment, benefits that might be partially passed through to the lessee/borrower, can result in lower net lease rates. But companies looking into leasing should do their homework before they take that to the bank.

Don't Believe It!

Don't believe that an equipment lease conveys unique tax benefits. It's not true!

We often hear radio ads touting the tax advantages of leasing over buying, for cars, for example. They tell us that we can deduct the payments on a lease, a unique advantage over buying. Well, guess what? It's not true.

The cost of a car, or any other asset, is tax-deductible if the asset is used for a tax-deductible purpose, regardless of how you paid for it. Any difference? In a lease you deduct the lease payments and in a purchase you deduct the depreciation and interest. In the end, the difference to you lies in which one cost you more money after taxes—and that will usually be the one that cost you more money *before* taxes.

One more variation is worth mentioning here. A company that owns its equipment and property outright but needs to raise money can sell its equipment to a financing source and then lease it back from the source, without anything changing physically. The company sells ownership of the property and then leases it for a period of years, just as if it were an original equipment lease like we've described above. Since the equipment is always used, the interest cost is usually higher, but the transaction effectively frees up cash invested in plant and equipment, to be used for another purpose.

Small Business Administration Will Guarantee Your Loan

A source long known to entrepreneurs and seasoned business owners is the Small Business Administration (SBA), an agency of the federal government that exists to support the growth of small business in this country. One of the ways the SBA does that is by helping small businesses get loans. In years past, the SBA was allocated money to make loans directly and to guarantee loans made by commercial banks. These days, all of the SBA's activity in this area goes to loan guarantees, not direct lending. Still, this is an excellent way to get long-term, inexpensive access to capital for growth.

The SBA guarantees a variety of loan types, one of which is

a term loan on business real estate. The owner of a company wanting to buy or build a factory to make its products can file an application with the SBA or, more commonly, any of the hundreds of banks designated "preferred SBA lenders." A small business owner typically has a good chance of obtaining such a loan, provided the company meets the bank's own lending standards, such as having collateral for the loan, an apparent ability to repay the loan in accordance with its terms, and so on. Interestingly, interest rates today are about the same as typical bank lending rates, or even a bit higher, despite the fact that the SBA guarantees the repayment of up to 90% of the loan, minimizing the bank's risk. Most authorized banks will assist business owners with their application or refer them to independent "loan packagers," who will complete the lengthy application paperwork for a fee, including helping the borrower understand things like cash forecasts and balance sheets.

Convertible Debt—The Transition from Debt to Equity

When a company needs to raise cash, there is always at some level the initial choice to be made: do we borrow money or do we sell stock in the company? Borrowing costs money in the form of interest payments, but selling equity dilutes the ownership interests of the present stockholders. In a period of economic misfortune, a company might have to sell a substantial piece of ownership to raise the money needed, while adequately compensating investors for taking the risk. Yet management doesn't want to be saddled with interest payments for a long time, particularly since a down time for a company usually means the interest rate it must pay to attract lenders is also high. What to do?

The answer for some companies is to sell debt that can be converted into equity at some point in the future when it's mutually beneficial to both the company and the lenders. This financing tool is called *convertible debt* or *convertible debentures*. By any name, a convertible bond is an instrument that

> **Bond** A negotiable instrument that is typically sold by pub-
> lic companies, pays interest quarterly, and is usually publicly
> traded during its life (just like company stock). Bonds are
> not collateralized, but they're often issued with insurance, purchased
> by the issuing company, that guarantees payment of principal and inter-
> est in the event the issuer defaults. This provision typically gives such
> bonds the highest investment grade rating, because it removes essen-
> tially all the ownership risk except interest rate fluctuation.
>
> **Debenture** A bond that may be sold publicly or privately, but that
> has no collateral to back it up except the strength of the issuing com-
> pany. These instruments are similar to bonds and are often enhanced
> by being convertible into the common stock of the issuer under cer-
> tain circumstances.

pays the lender interest only for some period of time, thus con-
serving the company's cash and enabling management to make
the most of its cash resources. Later, the lender may choose to
convert the debt into shares of stock at a predetermined conversion ratio. Result: the company stops paying high interest
and surrenders a reasonable amount of ownership.

Here's how it works. A company issues a convertible deben-
ture with provisions that call for interest to be paid periodically,
usually quarterly, but no principal. At some time in the future,
the bond is *callable*, meaning the company can buy it back
(usually at a premium over its face value) and retire it, in effect
paying off the loan. In the interim, the bond can be converted
into stock at any time, at a conversion ratio that is advanta-
geous to the company.

Capital Stock—Types and Uses

This section reviews some of the types of stock and how they're
used to finance a business.

Common Stock—Fundamental Ownership of the Corporation

Common stock is the basic form of ownership of a corporation.
In the classic scenario, a company's management issues stock
to investors in return for their cash and then uses the cash to

Terms of Borrowing	Duration of Loan	Collateral	Use	Cost
Revolving credit line	Credit line one-year renewable, but borrowing revolves indefinitely	Accounts receivable, inventory, other assets owned, not pledged elsewhere	Temporary cash needs; replacing the cash tied up in receivables and inventory until they can again become cash	Low
Accounts receivable loan	Credit line one-year renewable, but borrowing revolves indefinitely	Accounts receivable	Early access to cash tied up in receivables, similar to revolving credit line	Medium
Factoring	Invoice by invoice, 30-90 days, revolving as new sales are made	Accounts receivable	Getting cash from receivables, passing on risk of collection to the lender	High
Flooring	One to three years renewable, but borrowings revolve indefinitely	High-priced inventory, such as cars and boats	Financing showroom inventory of items for sale, which are also the collateral	Low
Term loans	Various annual terms depending on type of loan and life of asset financed-one to 30 years	Various, from collateral being purchased to all assets the company owns	Long-term purchases of assets or real estate or to provide capital for long-term projects to companies without adequate internal cash generation	Medium
Equipment loans and leasing	Three to five years, or longer, depending on life of the asset	The asset being acquired, or refinanced in case of sale-and-leaseback	Acquisition of large pieces of equipment or large amounts of equipment	Medium to High
Bonds	Variable, with lengths to 30 years and more	None, although some are mortgage-backed and others are insured against default	Major long-term projects for large companies, including expansion and acquisition programs	Low
Convertible debt	Variable, with lengths to 30 years and more	None, although conversion privilege adds value, especially in a good market	Major long-term projects for large companies, including expansion and acquisition programs	Low

Figure 11-1. Summary of common business borrowing methods

The Birth, Life, and Retirement of a Convertible Debenture

A convertible bond is issued with a conversion price of $25, meaning that a $1,000 bond can be converted into 40 shares of stock. But when the bond is issued, the market price of the stock is only $15. The lender will not consider converting, because buying shares on the open market would cost less than converting the bond. So the lender waits and collects interest on the loan, in this case 10% per year. Over time the company prospers. The stock price goes up to $30. Now the lender has a choice: collect $100 interest per year and in the future get repaid the $1,000 or convert the bond into 40 shares of stock and then sell the shares for $1,200 (40 X $30). The lender's decision will depend on his or her individual financial objectives, but there's a good chance the lender will convert. If so, the company ceases paying interest and does not have to repay the loan. It simply needs to issue 40 shares of stock to satisfy the conversion request and accept a slight dilution in its earnings per share. The lender gets a return greater than 10% on the money loaned. Everybody wins.

start and operate the business. A share of stock represents a unit of ownership of a company, but the size of that unit depends on the number of shares of stock issued. A small company owned by a handful of people might only have a few hundred shares outstanding, that is, owned by its stockholders. Microsoft, by contrast, has over five *billion* shares outstanding. So percentage of ownership is not just about how many shares you own; it's about how many shares everybody owns. Thus we arrive at a key observation of stock ownership: *the more shares there are, the less your shares are worth*. This is called *dilution*, as we discussed in Chapter 4.

Common stock is the basic ownership unit, as noted before. The common stockholder is the residual owner of the company's assets. That means the common stockholder gets all the remaining value when all the debts are settled, which may be a great deal or may be nothing. It is this risk/reward relationship that has enabled public stock ownership to become the best investment for growth in the long term—and also one of the riskiest investments in the short term.

Preferred Stock— Ownership with Perks ... and Limitations

There's a way for the investor to mitigate the risk without losing entirely the potential for appreciation. If a company needs additional equity capital and wants to avoid diluting

> **Key Term**
>
> **Common stock** Equity ownership in a corporation that entitles the stockholders to dividends and/or capital appreciation and the right to vote. In the event of liquidation, common stockholders have rights to corporate assets only after bondholders, holders of other debt, and preferred stockholders.

the value of its common stock, the choice might be to issue a separate class of shares, such as preferred stock. Preferred stock typically carries a stated dividend rate, in

---

Good for the Company, Bad for Shareholders

Issuing stock to raise cash helps the company, but it can hurt the shareholders.

Consider the example of Wonder Widget, our rapidly growing company. It is publicly owned now, under the understated symbol WOWI. The company is profitable, earning $1 million in net income last year. You own 1,000 shares, out of 500,000 outstanding. The company's earnings per share (EPS) were $2.00 ($1,000,000/500,000). The market thinks WOWI's shares are worth 20 times earnings (price/earnings ratio), meaning the company is valued at $20 million. Your shares would bring $40,000 (1,000 x $2 x 20) if you sold them today.

But the company is still growing, so the next year it sells some more stock, in a "secondary" stock offering: it sells 100,000 shares at $20 to raise $2 million in cash. WOWI is better off now, but how about you?

You still have your 1,000 shares and the company earns $1,050,000 that year, a 5% increase over the prior year. But since there are now 600,000 shares outstanding, EPS is down to $1.75 ($1,050,000/600,000). The market still thinks the company is worth 20 times earnings, so valuation is up to $21 million (20 x $1,050,000). Your shares, however, are now worth only $35,000 (1,000 x $1.75 x 20).

The company has more cash and is making more money. You did nothing different—and lost $5,000 in market value. That, dear reader, is *dilution*.

terms of percent of face value or dollars per share.

Preferred shares are indeed a separate class of stock, with privileges and restrictions different from common stock. And they're called preferred shares for good reason. When the board of directors decides to declare a dividend to the shareholders, the preferred shareholders must get their entire dividend, based on the stated dividend rate, before any dividends can be paid to the common shareholders. In some cases, the preferred shares are also *cumulative*, meaning that dividends not paid in one year accumulate as obligations of the company and must be paid up in full before any common stock dividends may be paid. For some companies, that can mean years of paying preferred dividends in full while giving common stockholders little or nothing.

> **Key Term**
>
> **Preferred stock** Equity ownership in a corporation that entitles the stockholders to a specific dividend before any dividends are paid on common stock. In the event of liquidation, preferred stockholders have rights to corporate assets after bondholders and holders of other debt but before common stockholders.

In the event of the dissolution of a company with both preferred and common shares outstanding, the cash raised from liquidating the assets is first used to repay all creditors. What's left goes to the stockholders, with the preferred stockholders coming first. If there's enough money to satisfy 100% of the preferred stockholders' claims, then the balance goes to the common stockholders. If there's not enough cash to satisfy both groups of owners, there's no pro-rata sharing between them. The preferred shareholders get all of theirs and the common shareholders get what is left, which may be nothing.

That, simply, is the meaning of the word "preferred."

So why doesn't every investor buy only preferred stock? The downside of preferred stock ownership is the limitation on participation in the extreme good fortune of the company. If a company does very well, it can declare a very handsome dividend for its common stockholders or give them additional shares (*stock dividends*) or both. Generally, however, such extras need not be paid to the preferred shareholders. The tradeoff for the preference is the restriction on enjoying the fruits of success. These restrictions have the effect of also restricting the market price appreciation of preferred shares, since they cannot participate in a company's dynamic growth as much as the common shares.

One feature sometimes added to preferred shares offsets this limitation. Some companies issue *convertible* preferred stock. These shares act like preferred shares until their owners decide to convert them, under provisions not unlike those built into the convertible debt discussed above. Once the holders convert their shares, the preference ends and they participate like other common stockholders, for better or worse. Typically, as with convertible debt, strong success is the best inducement to getting preferred shareholders to convert their shares. Once the preferred shares are converted, the company no longer has to reserve earnings for preferred dividends and can pay out those dollars as common stock dividends or retain them for expansion, repayment of debt, or any other corporate purpose.

Manager's Checklist for Chapter 11

❏ Borrowing rule no. 1: Lending is a very competitive business. Always shop for a loan, even if your favorite banker has made you an offer you can't refuse, unless saving money is not an important objective.

❏ Borrowing rule no. 2: Borrow short-term money only for short-term needs. Don't get caught with overdue loans because the long-term project they were financing has taken longer than expected to pay off.

❏ Perhaps the most expensive form of short-term borrowing for businesses is factoring, the sale of accounts receivable to the lender: rates can go as high as 5% a month and paperwork requirements are substantial.

❏ Leasing equipment and buying equipment on installments

are both ways to finance the acquisition of equipment. They differ mostly in the strength of the lien held by the lender, the size of the monthly payments, and the net borrowing cost. Again, shop around.

❑ Dilution can lower the value of your investment even when things are going well. Pay attention to the potential dilutive effects of the actions of any company in which you hold stock. The most common examples are stock options and new stock sales.

Attracting Outside Investors: The Entrepreneur's Path

The United States is without question the entrepreneurial capital of the world.

More people start businesses here than anywhere else on the planet, and more of them succeed than anywhere else. Of course, it's also likely true that more of them fail here than anywhere else. But they try, because that's the kind of capitalistic system we have. People know that if they try and succeed, they will be rewarded both financially and socially. Even if they try and fail, they know they will not be ostracized. On the contrary, they might even get another chance. Some entrepreneurs tell stories of several failures before they ultimately became successful, and they tell those stories with understandable pride—pride in their own perseverance and achievement and pride in a capitalistic economy and political system that not only permit but encourage that kind of effort.

Many start-up businesses, notably the technology-related companies that were started so prolifically over the past decade, have needed some financial support from outside

Key Term **Entrepreneur** A businessperson who starts a company with the intention from the beginning of growing it to be much larger than would be necessary to simply provide an income to the owner and (typically) selling it at some point—to the public through a stock offering or to another company—for a substantial profit.

investors in order to get started and get their first products to market. Many others needed outside investors to expand their companies.

There are many sources for investment capital potentially available to the promising or proven entrepreneur. Sometimes the money comes from the founder's own pocket at first, from savings or borrowing against the house or raiding the kids' college fund. But often the money comes from others who have heard about the entrepreneur's dream and want to be a part of it.

This chapter is an overview of the sources of investment capital for the entrepreneur, from the first dollar invested to the last dollar before the entrepreneur sells what he or she has built. The discussion follows generally the order in which the entrepreneur will tap those sources of capital, from the first to the last. Keep in mind that a particular company may not need all these stages in order to reach profitability and cash self-sufficiency, and some will need them all, depending on the complexity of the enterprise and the difficulty in establishing a successful market position.

So, when an entrepreneur wants to start a company and needs more money than he or she has in the bank, these are the places to go knocking with that exciting business plan in hand. These are the investors.

The Start-up Company: Seed Money and Its Sources

Regardless of how difficult it is to do, the entrepreneur starting a company from scratch must almost always put up the initial money from his or her own resources. This is so for several reasons:

- There may be no one else who believes the idea can work until the entrepreneur proves it and then can attract investments.
- The founder wants to keep as much of the stock ownership as possible and believes, or at least hopes, to succeed without any outside funding.
- Potential investors have suggested to the entrepreneur that they may invest, but only if he or she first invests meaningful personal funds. This is referred to as having "skin in the game." (Don't ask how the analogy arose; I don't think either of us wants to know!)

So, the entrepreneur calls on savings, talks his or her spouse into refinancing the house, or asks the parents, aunts and uncles, and very close friends to invest. Such sources are typically, and usually accurately, referred to as "friends and family." These are usually good sources for initial capital (*seed money*), because they have known the entrepreneur a long time and have faith in him or her or because they feel enough empathy for the entrepreneur's efforts to be willing to take more risks than more objective investors might.

This initial injection of money enables two important changes to take place:

- The entrepreneur becomes a founder, a president and CEO who now has the opportunity to begin to prove that his or her idea is good enough to attract investors.
- The entrepreneur can move from idea to reality. He or she can set up an office, begin development of the business, hire employees, and create a business plan to serve as the brochure for the next round in the continuing search for capital.

Professional Investors: Angels on a Mission

Once the start-up company has a little momentum, perhaps with a prototype of an invention or a product, some interested

> **Key Term**
>
> **Angel investor** An individual who invests in start-up or emerging companies for his or her own account, rather than as part of a formal organization or company. Usually an individual with some personal wealth and prior management or investing experience, or both. Sometimes called simply "angels," these individuals may seek out investment opportunities on their own, or they may join groups of other angels in an informal "angel network," sort of like an early stage investment club, to find opportunities that appeal to several members of the group.

potential buyers, or even a few paying customers, the founder may be in a position to tell a compelling story to potential investors. These may be individuals who have made some money beyond what they need for their own personal and business use and have set aside some of that money for investing in other people's new ideas. These investors are often called *angels* because they will often come to the rescue of the entrepreneur and make an investment when no one else is able or willing.

Angels don't do this because they are foolish, but because they have a greater risk tolerance than other folks and because their background often makes them uniquely able and willing to assist a start-up company with ideas, introductions, and advice—in addition to money.

What Angel Investors Want to See

So, how does an entrepreneur attract the interest of angels? These potential investors typically are attracted by the following:

- A reasonably well written business plan outlining the concept and the investment premise
- A founder with sufficient business management experience to convince the investor that he or she can carry out the promise of the plan
- A demonstration in some form of the product or service, to allow angels to judge the likelihood of the entrepreneur achieving what the business plan defines as success

- An organization with a reasonable management team in place and ready to carry out the plan, perhaps some interested prospective buyers, and maybe even a few customers to help prove market potential
- As many of the things on the venture capitalists' list (in the next section) as possible.

The first professional investor to take a chance on a company will typically be able to obtain a substantial percentage of ownership in the company in return for an investment. The early-stage investor commands a strong ownership position because he or she is taking a chance very early in the game, when the risk of loss is correspondingly higher than later, when some parts of the idea have been proven.

These first-round professional investors will often take an active role in helping the company grow. This first outside investor will serve on the board of directors and/or advisory board. He or she may help the founder attract key executives to the management team or, if the need is acute and the company is not ready for high-level employees just yet, strategic management consultants. The investor will typically provide guidance; many are seasoned executives or entrepreneurs.

For some companies, these early-stage investors will provide all the outside capital needed to reach profitability. A start-up company that does not require huge infusions of cash for research and development may be able to build sales momentum early on and use much of its investors' money to establish market position and put a sales organization in place. This will hasten the climb to profits and self-sufficiency and enable the investors to earn a good return on their money in a short time.

This is not the normal situation, however, as start-up companies will typically take three to five years or more before their investors can convert their investment into cash again. The more typical start-up company that requires investor capital will need several infusions or rounds of capital before it is self-sufficient in terms of cash flow. Early-round money may be needed to prove the soundness of the business concept, to begin the development of the product or service, and to start building the organization.

Perhaps most important to the founder who will need more money as the company gains momentum, first-round investors may facilitate introductions to later-stage investors who might be willing to invest larger amounts of money, based on the company's results, thus enabling further progress toward profitability and a handsome return for all. Prominent among these next-stage investors are the money managers known as *venture capitalists*.

Venture Capitalists: What You Need to Know to Attract Them

When more money is needed than the angels can provide or when the angels want others to invest to support their early stakes, a young company may seek out the institutional investors, the folks known as *venture capitalists* (VCs to those inclined to buzzwords).

The venture capitalists' job is to evaluate the investment opportunity, make the investing decision, and then monitor the investment's performance over time, with the hope of selling the investors' shares at a profit for the investors (and themselves, since these folks usually accumulate shares for their personal accounts along the way, sometimes by direct investment and sometimes in the form of options or warrants for their services).

Venture capitalist (VC) A member of a firm that invests in emerging companies, many in start-up mode, typically for others rather than for their own account, often by starting an investment fund and convincing other institutions, corporations, or wealthy individuals to passively invest in the fund and then finding good opportunities for investing. VCs also provide assistance in guiding the growth and subsequent funding of their portfolio companies until they are either sold to other companies or sold to the public in a public offering of shares (see "The Initial Public Offering" below).

What Venture Capitalists Want to See

Venture capitalists are attracted by the following:

- All the things on the angels' list (above)
- A polished business plan with solid thinking in regard to all the key success factors, the inhibitors to success, and the advantages of the proposed product or service
- A potential market that is very large, so that even a small market share will produce a big sales volume
- The ability of the new company to gain a foothold in the market that will inhibit competitors
- A distinct competitive advantage over all the alternatives that customers have or might have in the future
- For a technology company, a compelling new technology that is difficult for potential competitors to copy, circumvent, or make obsolete
- The potential to grow to a valuation at least 10 times beyond the valuation at which the investors purchased their shares within a reasonable timeframe, typically three to seven years

Valuation is the term used to define the proposed total market value of the venture, which will in turn define the amount of ownership interest the investors will receive for a given dollar investment. This valuation is an estimate of a company that typically has no value in traditional terms—sales and earnings. Therefore, it's as much a negotiation as a calculation.

For example, a venture may be valued at $5 million by the founder, who might want to raise $2.5 million. The founder's calculation might go as shown in Figure 12-1.

The venture capitalist,

> **Key Term**
>
> **Valuation** The proposed total market value of a venture, which defines the amount of ownership interest any investor will receive for investing. Since this valuation is an estimate of a company that typically has no value in traditional terms (sales and earnings), it's as much a negotiation between the company and venture capitalists as a calculation.

Value of the venture before the investment of $2.5M ("*pre*-money valuation")	$5 million
Value of the venture after the investment of $2.5M ("*post*-money valuation") (= pre-money valuation + investment)	$7.5 million
Value of the investor's $2.5M in terms of ownership percentage ($2.5M/$7.5M)	33 1/3%
Percent of the firm the entrepreneur offers to sell for $2.5M	33 1/3%

Figure 12-1. The entrepreneur's calculation

Value of the venture before the investment of $2.5M ("*pre*-money valuation")	$2.5 million
Value of the venture after the investment of $2.5M ("*post*-money valuation") (= pre-money valuation + investment)	$5 million
Value of the investor's $2.5M in terms of ownership percentage ($2.5/$5.0M)	50%
Percent of the firm the investor wants to own for $2.5M	50%

Figure 12-2. The venture capitalist's calculation

however, might look at it somewhat differently, as shown in Figure 12-2.

The difference between the two views is one of perspective. Since both are estimating future value in their negotiating, neither is right and neither is wrong. The person in the stronger negotiating position will usually get more of what he or she wants. When a company approaches a VC firm for an initial investment, the firm is usually in the stronger position. Once the company has proven its ideas, attracted customers, and perhaps even piqued the interest of other VC firms, the founder may be in a stronger negotiating position.

Venture capital firms typically prefer to keep a low profile. Despite that preference, their names are published in books eagerly purchased by entrepreneurs and they receive hundreds of unsolicited business plans every year, only a fraction of which ever get read. It's generally acknowledged, although never stated as an absolute, that a business plan has little chance of getting serious attention

---

Negotiating with Clout

A company that has attracted the interest of VC firms may be in a very strong position to negotiate funding. While serving as the CFO of such a company, I once participated in a board of directors meeting where the outside VC interest was so strong that the company actually turned money away, effectively rationing the next investment opportunity to those firms they felt could be most beneficial to the company's strategic agenda. Now, *that's* my idea of negotiating leverage!

---

unless it has been introduced by someone known to the venture capital firm, someone whose opinion they value or at least feel comfortable with. Thus, when it comes to getting attention from these investors, it's often truly a matter of who you know.

Venture capital firms account for only a small portion of all the investment funds poured into new businesses every year. Entrepreneurs who have had VC investors on their boards tell a mixed bag of stories ranging from masterfully insightful guidance to self-serving decisions designed more to protect the VC investment than to foster the venture's success. Yet because of their reputation, their ready pools of cash, and their skill in identifying and backing some of the most successful start-ups in memory, nearly every entrepreneur who starts a new venture seeks or at least covets the views, the money, and the support of venture capitalists.

For their part, in spite of their skill at evaluating new ventures, these investors expect to be wrong most of the time. In fact, the traditional wisdom says they will lose money on four of five investments they make, but getting a 10-to-1 return on the

Avoid the Top 10 Lies

Guy Kawasaki, CEO of Garage Technology Ventures, warns against the following statements that entrepreneurs most commonly use with venture capitalists.

1. **Our projections are conservative.** Venture capitalists know that entrepreneurs are optimistic. They won't take your projections at face value.

2. **ABC [a consulting firm] predicts our market will swell to $X by 200X.** Refrain from giving numbers. Anybody can predict almost anything.

3. **XYZ [a huge company] is about to sign a sales contract with us.** Entrepreneurs may interpret even a polite rejection as a sign of true interest. VCs know better.

4. **Key employees will join us as soon as we get funded.** VCs have telephones and can call those key prospective employees.

5. **We have first-mover advantage.** Two problems. One, first-mover advantage doesn't matter, not as much as "first to scale." Two, it's easy for VCs to check out claims to an advantage.

6. **Several VCs are already interested.** VCs can check out this claim; if it's untrue, you lose a lot of credibility.

7. **_____ [a big industry leader] is too slow to be a threat.** VCs will read in such a statement a lack of awareness of the market.

8. **We're glad the bubble has burst.** OK, so it's good that investors and entrepreneurs are more rational and realistic, but what sane entrepreneur would be pleased that investment money is harder to obtain?

9. **Our patents make our business defensible.** Be realistic: outside of medical devices and biotechnology, patents mean very little. If an idea is worth money, somebody will copy it.

10. **All we have to do is get 1% of the market.** Leave the worst-case scenario to the VCs. Aim at a figure you consider realistic— and show how you intend to hit it.

Source: www.garage.com/guy/speeches/Lies_of_Entrepreneurs.pdf

fifth makes the whole thing worthwhile. If you think about it, would you make your living doing something that you expected to fail at 80% of the time? Perhaps that's why these investors ask for *and typically get* the valuation leverage they ask for, even when it seems so unfair to the hard-working founder.

The Initial Public Offering—Heaven or Hell?

As we've already mentioned, the "pot of gold at the end of the rainbow," the goal of long-term strategies for the entrepreneur who doesn't want to run a company for the rest of his or her working life is to sell it for a lot of money and retire to a beach in Tahiti or a golf course in Florida. While there are several ways to do that, selling the company to the investing public through a public offering of stock will typically bring the largest return to the sellers. The first time the company sells its shares in the public market, it's called the *initial public offering* (IPO). So, for the classic entrepreneur, the IPO is the ultimate exit strategy.

Unfortunately for the entrepreneur with beach-front dreams, the IPO isn't quite as simple as selling all the shares and walking away dragging a bag full of money. The U.S. government, through the Securities and Exchange Commission (SEC), long ago decided

> **Key Term**
>
> **Initial public offering (IPO)** The first sale of equity in a company to the public, generally in the form of shares of common stock, through an investment banking firm.

that was a bad idea because too many owners were selling a pig in a poke to unwary public investors who found out too late their shares weren't worth what they paid for them. Nowadays all the owners, including the professional investors, will remain owners after the IPO and their fortunes will rise and fall with the public stock price, making everyone interested in the same goal, consistent price appreciation.

The SEC aside, the prospect of selling shares over time, along with the likelihood that the company's continued success will raise the stock price still further, makes the IPO the preferred exit strategy, if the company can get it. That's a *big* "if," because not every company that has investor backing makes a big enough splash to interest investment bankers. Remember the eight in 10 companies that don't make it? And the one in 10 that makes it big? Well, that means that roughly 90% of the start-ups that get funded by professional investors will not likely be good enough to become IPO stocks—the actual numbers are even more daunting. And of those that do, many will deliver less stellar performance than projected in their IPO offering literature. Some of them will sink to market prices below their IPO price, while others will languish with modest returns and sort of disappear into the haze without ever making a significant impact on the market.

CAUTION!

Don't Count on an IPO

It would be simple if any company could just go public. Unfortunately, it takes more than mere desire—and few succeed. The most likely candidates for an IPO are companies in industries that are hot—according to the whims of the stock market—and companies that are expected to reach revenues upwards of $100 million quickly.

Still, the exhilarating prospects of making it big in that breathtaking game gives company owners hope. Along the way, they are aided by the coaches and advisors, the investors, consultants, accountants, lawyers, and a variety of others, because everyone wants to play in the big game. And everyone believes it can happen to them—and no one knows for sure, until they take their shot.

Strategic Investors: The Path to a Different Party

So let's do a little guessing here. There are an awful lot of companies that start up every year; even if only 5% of them stay in business, that would still be a big number. If only 10% of them

hit it big, that would still be far more than the annual IPO statistics. What happens to all the rest—the companies that are successful but don't go public?

Well, many of them simply become successful privately
owned companies; in fact, many of the most successful companies in this country are quietly owned by private interests. Yet
there are still a large number of companies that have great
ideas but still don't raise venture capital money. Many of them
were started by entrepreneurs who had the same dream of a
rich exit as their IPO counterparts. Do they just give up and go
home? Not by a long shot. Many of these companies go the
other route—teaming up with an existing company that appreci-
ates the value of their ideas and hopes to improve its own business through by the success of the start-up.

Such companies often become *strategic investors*, investing
in a promising start-up in return for both stock ownership and
the first opportunity to receive the benefit of the start-up's inno-
vations. They may want the rights to sell the venture's products
as their own, to incorporate the venture's products into their
own, or to ultimately buy the start-up company and merge it
into their business. That benefit is mutual, if it's done right:

- The venture gets access to the technical expertise of the
  larger company to help it solve issues more easily.
- The investor gets innovation it likely is not nimble enough
  to create by itself, except at an exorbitant cost.
- The venture gets a partner with much more marketing
  muscle than it would have alone, perhaps even getting its
  products into the strategic partner's sales force offering,
  producing a built-in customer.
- The investor gets to offer new products, perhaps including
  state-of-the-art technology that it didn't know how to
  develop or wasn't prepared to take the risk of trying to
  develop.
- The investor may be able to purchase this company and
  its products and innovation for a fraction of the cost of

buying an established company, if it even could find an established company willing to be acquired.

Acquisition: The Strategic Exit

Let's suppose you're the founder/CEO of a company that did-n't get angel funding, didn't get VC funding, didn't get strategic partner funding, and *still* managed to build a company that is making it on its own. The company is self-sufficient in terms of cash flow and modestly profitable, but it just doesn't have enough resources to take full advantage of its market position. Let's further assume that your company's not going to be an IPO candidate because it's just not exciting enough to sizzle the pages of a prospectus. Finally, let's suppose the company was built on some innovative technology that's like-ly to be seriously challenged in a few years. This is a pretty fair assumption, just because technology moves pretty fast these days, particularly if a company has demonstrated there's a ready, profitable market for it.

Many founders will look at the prospect of running such a company for five or 10 more years to just make an adequate living and say, "No more!" Others will be ready to go the distance, but fearful of their chances against bigger, well-financed competitors and worried that they might lose it all. Their options? Fold the tent and go home, hang on and hope for the best, or find a very big brother to protect the company from intruders.

In financial circles, finding a big brother doesn't mean going to some charity event or calling long-lost relatives. It means finding a large company that will acquire the young company and perhaps be willing to pay off the owner/managers after some transition period or offer them jobs running their company from inside the newly acquired big brother.

Without a strategic partner, the management team must find a prospective buyer and then convince that company that acquiring it would be a good idea. They might do that by hiring an investment banker or by initiating their own search, but the idea is to find a friendly 800-pound gorilla they know and like before an 800-pounder they don't know and don't like arrives on the block. The young company will be looking for the following:

- the possibility of making a friendly deal, with a better price for the stock held by the owners than might be available later, in more challenging times,
- jobs for the company's employees, including the CEO if desired, which might not be so easy later with an unfriendly buyer, and
- the ability to pick the time to look for a deal, when the company looks its best, things are on an up trend, there's cash in the bank, and it isn't facing any immediate threat.

By contrast, the potential acquirer will have a different list, which might include the following:

- maintaining or increasing a growth rate that stockholders have come to expect, particularly if the acquisition is in a growth area expected to be "hot" very soon,
- protecting itself from inroads into its market by younger companies with the kind of innovative products it lacks,
- putting excess plant capacity to work by building products for the young company at favorable incremental cost because it's already paying for the capacity,
- putting excess cash to work earning a better long-term return than it can earn sitting in the bank, or
- developing complementary products (e.g., lawn tools for a lawnmower company or computer printers for a computer company).

There are some distinct differences in an acquisition under these circumstances and the kind of deal that might be made with a strategic investor. For example, a company that acquires a venture rather than investing in it early on doesn't bear the added cost *and risk* of nurturing the young company to self-sufficiency. For coming late to the party, however, it will likely pay much more for the company now, because it has less risk and a higher certainty of a good return on investment. And the selling stockholders are generally entitled to a better price because they rode out the rough times carrying all the risk.

Of course, like any acquisition transaction, the outcome will be the result of negotiation more than calculation and logic, as each party tries to present his or her case and convince the other to accept it or something close to it. For this reason, CEOs wishing to buy or sell will typically enlist the services of negotiating experts, such as investment bankers, mergers and acquisitions (M&A) consultants, or lawyers skilled in deal making.

Manager's Checklist for Chapter 12

❏ Angel investors are often the first step for entrepreneurs to find outside financing, after they have exhausted their "friends and family" resources. Angels will typically accept the highest risk and make the smaller investments that very early stage companies need to get started.

❏ Venture capital investors are often the next stage for the entrepreneur. They will invest larger amounts, but will typically ask for larger stakes in the company and expect it to make more progress before they will invest.

❏ Valuation of the company when it is not yet earning a profit, or even bringing in revenues, is a challenging task that is crucial to the company getting investment capital, yet the lack of real data typically reduces the decision to negotiation rather than calculation.

❏ While the initial public offering is often the "pot of gold at the end of the rainbow," few companies realize the dream of achieving that goal. Many more are acquired by strategic partners, sold once they have matured, or simply run under private ownership.

Index

Index